PARADISE
ROAD

THE SCREENPLAY OF THE FILM
WRITTEN BY BRUCE BERESFORD

BASED ON THE STORY
BY DAVID GILES AND MARTIN MEADER

A Buzz Book
St. Martin's Press
New York

Book Design by Gretchen Achilles

Web Site: http://www.buzzmag.com
Web Site: http://www.foxsearchlight.com

ISBN 0-312-17200-1

First Buzz Book Edition: May 1997
10   9   8   7   6   5   4   3   2   1

FOREWORD

Ideas for films have come to me in many different ways. I've cut news items from papers and magazines, read novels and seen plays, had stories told to me, and even been sent good material from Hollywood studios. *Paradise Road* is unique for me in having as its basis a piece of music.

In 1991 I was played a rather bad-quality cassette of a memorial concert that was held in Perth, Western Australia. The music was an arrangement, for voices, of the Largo from Dvorak's *New World* symphony. I was told that this music had been sung in a Japanese prison camp. The delicacy and beauty of the arrangement overwhelmed me, and I determined to find out all I could about the story behind it.

Quite a few survivors from the camps are still alive, nearly all very elderly. I interviewed a number of them in Australia, England, and America. They had all been either captured after the fall of Singapore (January 1942) or, in the case of the Dutch, been interned when the Japanese overran the former Dutch East Indies. They spent nearly four years, until the end of the war, as prisoners.

I learned that the two women responsible for the choir were both English: Nora Chambers, a former violinist, and Margaret Dryburgh, who had been a missionary. I was never really able to discover a vast amount about their personalities, but I did use the snippets I gleaned as a basis for the characters of Adrienne Pargiter (Glenn Close) and Margaret Drummond (Pauline Collins). Similarly, the other characters were evoked (I can't say with what degree of success) often from mere hints—a snobbish English lady and her daughter, an Australian nurse, an American, an Irishwoman, a young model, a forthright nun, a Dutch girl, and so on—that enabled me to imagine what it would be like if they were all mixed up in a camp together, what they would say to one another, what the conflicts would be, et cetera. I read numerous books (some of them translated from Dutch and Japanese) and diaries (including a number of unpublished ones deposited in the Imperial War Museum in London) that gave me, I think, enough information to be able to re-create life in a P.O.W. camp in Sumatra, 1942–1945.

—BRUCE BERESFORD
Sydney, Australia
1997

OVERVIEW

During the early years of World War II Japanese troops swept rapidly through China and Southeast Asia. Among the countries they occupied were British and Dutch colonies. Tens of thousands of Europeans were captured and imprisoned for the duration of the war.

The women in the story were captured on the island of Sumatra either after fleeing Singapore by boat and being sunk by Japanese planes, or, in the case of the Dutch, being Sumatran residents.

There were a number of camps similar to the one portrayed in *Paradise Road*. Conditions varied, depending on the character and administration of the Japanese Camp Commander, but, even at their best, they were atrocious. Overall, between 30% and 40% of the women died.

Paradise Road is inspired by actual events. A women's choir *was* formed at one of the camps at the instigation of two remarkable Englishwomen. The music survived the war and can be performed in the film precisely as it was in fact.

The script is the result of extensive research with survivors of a number of camps. Diaries and recollections, published and unpublished, were a great help in ensuring authenticity.

Most of the characters involved in the script are inspired by actual people, although detailed information was difficult to obtain because of the passing of time and fading memories, so there is a great deal of invention—this is not a documentary about camp life but a feature based on a little-known arena of the second world war. It is a story of suffering and heroism that rivals, I believe, any widely known stories of the war.

—BRUCE BERESFORD
March 1, 1996

CHARACTERS

Adrienne PARGITER *British. 35. Wife of tea planter. Ex-violinist.*

Margaret DRUMMOND *British. 55. Missionary/musician.*

Susan MACARTHY *Australian. 26. Nurse.*

Rosemary LEIGHTON-JONES *British. 27. Model.*

Dr. VERSTAK *German. 47. Wife of White Russian doctor.*

Topsy MERRITT *American. 36. Wife of Singapore businessman.*

Mrs. O'RIORDEN *Irish. 38.*

Mrs. TIPPLER *English. 40.*

Mrs. E. A. ROBERTS *English. 58. Snobby wife of head of Singapore PWD.*

Celia ROBERTS *English. 30. Daughter of above.*

Helen Van PRAAGH *Dutch. 19.*

Sister WILHELMINA *Dutch. 35.*

Mrs. DICKSON *English. 39.*

Mrs. PIKE *English. 42.*

EDNA *Australian nurse. 27.*

OGGI *Australian nurse. 27.*

BETT *Australian. 27. Army secretary.*

WING *Chinese. 44.*

Michele ROUETTE *French. 34.*

Siobhan O'RIORDEN *Irish. 15. Daughter of Mrs. O'Riorden.*

MILLIE *Chinese. 33.*

Mrs. CRONJE *Dutch. 42.*

Sister ANNA *Dutch nun. 28.*

Antoinette VAN PRAAGH *Dutch. 15.*

Ann LORD *30. Journalist.*

Colonel HIROTA *Japanese. 43. Camp commandant.*

Captain TANAKA *Japanese. 32. Kempei-tai (Secret Police) representative.*

The SNAKE *Japanese. 35. Camp guard.*

Mr. MOTO *Japanese. 31. Guard who resembles fictional detective.*

RAGS *Japanese. 26. Untidy guard.*

BORIS *Japanese. 33. Guard who resembles Boris Karloff.*

LOFTY *Japanese. 22. Tall guard.*

INTERPRETER *Japanese. 37. Nervous schoolteacher.*

EXT. RAFFLES HOTEL. SINGAPORE. EARLY EVENING. 1942.

A wide shot of the hotel with the words "Raffles Hotel, Singapore, 10th of February, 1942." superimposed on the screen.

A DANCE BAND can be heard, mixed in with the sound of chatter and laughter. A girl VOCALIST is singing Noël Coward's "Mad About the Boy."

VOCALIST

Mad about the boy,
It's, I know, stupid to be mad about the boy
I'm so ashamed of it
But must admit
The sleepless nights I've had about the boy

INT. RAFFLES HOTEL. BALLROOM. NIGHT.

The large room is packed with COUPLES dancing. The WOMEN mostly young and attractive, the MEN mostly SOLDIERS and nearly all officers— they are a mixture of British and Australians. There is also a sprinkling of OLDER MEN (over forty) and their wives. These are locals, working in Colonial administration or the rubber, tea, tin, or oil industries.

WAITERS—Malays, Chinese, Indians—move among the guests in spotless traditional clothes, taking orders, dispensing food and drink.

The large ORCHESTRA at one end of the room is dressed in white tuxedos. The Coward song continues.

VOCALIST

Walking down the street,
His eyes look out at me from people that
I meet,
I can't believe it's true
But when I'm blue,
In some strange way I'm glad about the boy.

A young Australian Lieutenant (BILL SEARY) approaches a GROUP of YOUNG WOMEN and asks SUSAN to dance. She is 25, pretty, with a shy manner. They join the LARGE CROWD on the dance floor.

BILL
Excuse me . . . Excuse me . . . So where are you from?

He speaks with a well-educated Australian accent.

SUSAN

Mudgee.

BILL

A country girl. I knew it.

SUSAN

How?

BILL

They're always shy. You blushed when I asked you to dance.

SUSAN

I did not. It's just hot . . .

BILL

Have you a boyfriend?

SUSAN

Yes. Oh, no, no. Well, I had one but he's in Egypt or somewhere.

BILL

Egypt? Well forget him. He's probably chasing some dusky maiden 'round the pyramids by now.

(Bill and Susan laugh)

Nearby, an extremely beautiful girl, in her mid-20s, is dancing with an aristocratic-looking man of around 30. He has the rank of captain and wears the uniform of the Malay Volunteers. ROSEMARY AND DENNIS LEIGHTON-JONES. Both are English and speak in refined upper-class accents.

ROSEMARY

You know what they call this dance?

DENNIS

No idea.

ROSEMARY

The Crush.

DENNIS

Do they? Well, I'm not really complaining.

Dennis lowers Rosemary in dance move and pulls her back up.

DENNIS

You're so beautiful, Rosemary.

2

ROSEMARY

So are you.

DENNIS

You can't say that. Can you? Men aren't . . . I am not beautiful.

ROSEMARY

Yes you are.

INT. RAFFLES HOTEL DINING ROOM. NIGHT.

VOCALIST

I'm feeling quite insane
And young again
And all because I'm mad about the boy

PARGITER

We've got everyone Churchill can spare. Thousands of bloody Australians drinking the place dry!

The dining room is vast. Tables with small individual lights and fine linen and silver are separated by potted palms. The room is packed with DINERS. WAITERS scurry busily but unobtrusively back and forth.

The DINERS sit at the tables arranged around the dance floor.

One table of eight DINERS includes ADRIENNE PARGITER, a handsome woman in her 30s, and her husband, WILLIAM PARGITER, a tea planter in his late 40s. The other guests are MR. AND MRS. PIKE and MR. AND MRS. DICKSON, and an American couple, MARTY and TOPSY MERRITT. The MEN work for the Colonial civil service or the tea and rubber industries. MERRITT is head of a pineapple packing plant. The couples are all in their 30s/early 40s. The WOMEN are elegantly dressed—perhaps somewhat over-dressed—with jewelry and heavily applied makeup. The MEN are wearing either light tropical suits (with ties) or tuxedos. Only ADRIENNE is plainly if neatly dressed, and wears no jewelry apart from her wedding ring.

PARGITER is answered by DICKSON, a bald Colonial with a large mustache.

DICKSON

All to fight tiny little Japanese chaps wearing spectacles. They're all cross-eyed, you know. Can't aim their damn guns!

He laughs. MRS. DICKSON snorts in agreement. She downs her G&T, then looks around for a waiter to order another. ADRIENNE looks disbelievingly from one man at the table to the next.

3

PARGITER

At night they can't see at all!

MRS. DICKSON

Do they all have white sticks and guide dogs?

MRS. PIKE

Phyllis, it's true, really. Cyril remember that Japanese gardener we had? He had glasses as thick as . . . as . . .

MRS. DICKSON

Bottom of a gin bottle?

MRS. PIKE

Yes.

MR. PIKE

It's certainly a fact their weapons are useless. My Godfather, all they can make are tin toys and cameras that don't work!

ADRIENNE

If you don't mind me saying so—even if you do—I don't think I've ever heard such a total load of poppycock. They've conquered most of Asia!

The MEN all laughingly protest.

4

TOPSY

And those "little Japanese chaps"—you heard of a place called Pearl Harbor?

TOPSY speaks with an educated Southern accent.

ADRIENNE

Exactly.

PARGITER

My dear Topsy—Adrienne—Pearl Harbor was a surprise . . . a sneak attack. *We're* all ready and waiting for 'em.

MARTY

I hope you're right.

INT. HOTEL BALLROOM. NIGHT.

A group of girls (all AUSTRALIAN NURSES, though this is not yet apparent) are by the bar area. A number of AUSTRALIAN SOLDIERS are chatting to them. One soldier brings EDNA back from the dance floor. He moves away to get some drinks.

EDNA

Thanks. Ooh.

OGGI

That one came on a bit strong, eh?

EDNA

Sort of. He's nice . . . I just don't reckon he's got too much upstairs.

A SOLDIER arrives and begins to lead OGGI to the dance floor. She turns back to EDNA as she begins to move away.

SOLDIER

Come on, Oggi.

OGGI

It's what they've got downstairs that really counts.

EDNA is puzzled by the remark. She looks toward her returning SOLDIER and takes the punch he offers her. She looks up, aware of a low whistling sound.

The whistling sound grows louder, gradually overwhelming the orchestra and vocalist. Then the "crump" of a shell landing somewhere in the distance, though not too far away. Another follows, slightly closer. The ORCHESTRA stops for a moment. There is a silence, then the music and dancing resume.

5

VOCALIST

VOCALIST
This dream that pains me and enchains me
But I can't because I'm mad about the boy

INT. HOTEL DINING ROOM. NIGHT.

The chatter in the dining room has also ceased for a moment, then resumes. The DINERS exchange glances but make no comment. MRS. DICKSON downs her second G&T.

DICKSON
How's that son of yours, Pargiter? Where is he? Westminster?

At another table, a large woman in her fifties, MRS. ROBERTS, is sitting with her husband, ROBBIE, and daughter, CELIA—a girl of around thirty. MRS. ROBERTS is clutching a small DOG. They all react to the sound of the explosion.

MRS. ROBERTS
Robbie! What was that?

ROBBIE
Just target practice, I expect, my dear.

MRS. ROBERTS
Target practice? At night? Oh . . . Celia, run upstairs and get my wrap, will you, dear?

CELIA
You're wearing it, Mummy.

MRS. ROBERTS
What . . . *(she looks down at the shawl around her shoulders)* Oh . . . Oh, so I am. I was just confused.

INT. HOTEL BALLROOM. NIGHT.

A GROUP of BRITISH OFFICERS march purposefully through the ballroom. The officer in charge is COLONEL DOWNES, a short and stocky man in his 40s. He wears a neat military mustache and has a dark tan.
    The DANCERS fall back. The music stops. DOWNES mounts the podium and stands next to the band leader. TWO JUNIOR OFFICERS unfold a map and hold it up—it shows Singapore at the end of the Malayan peninsula and surrounding detail.

6

DOWNES

Pardon me, please, ladies and gentlemen.

On the map he indicates an area a few miles north of the city.

DOWNES

Pardon me please. Pardon. Good evening, ladies and gentlemen. I'm sorry to disturb this evening's entertainment but I have some rather unhappy news. The Japanese have now crossed the Jahora Strait and have broken through our lines.

A quick murmur runs through the crowd. ROSEMARY LEIGHTON-JONES clutches her HUSBAND. DOWNES' manner remains crisp and unemotional.

DOWNES

... and their guns have the city in range ...

More explosions land nearby.

DOWNES

... as you can hear.

DICKSON stands and calls out ...

DICKSON

But Colonel, only today the *Straits Times* reported that the Japanese were being driven back ...

DOWNES

Yes, well I'm afraid, sir, the only true thing you can read in the newspapers are the cricket scores.

Laughter runs across the room. More shells land, not far away. SOLDIERS are opening the windows to prevent them being blown in by bomb blasts. They press themselves against the wall as a bright flash lights up the distance. In the distance, sirens begin to wail.

DOWNES

Don't worry, this hotel will be perfectly safe.

ROSEMARY

(to Dennis) Why?

DENNIS indicates with a glance that DOWNES is about to explain.

DOWNES

(continuing)—as I'm sure the Japanese High Command will want to stay here and avail themselves of the facilities ...

7

A murmur goes around the room as the significance of this statement strikes THE CROWD. ROSEMARY shoots an apprehensive look to DENNIS. THE GROUP from the dining room, now standing in the entrance of the ballroom, are taken aback.

DOWNES
The city will fall within a few days. All European women and children are to leave immediately. . . .

SUSAN looks toward her FRIENDS.

SUSAN
He can't mean us! They'll need us.

She addresses the remark to her friend Oggi, who is standing with her partner a few feet away.

DOWNES
All soldiers are to return to their units. Good luck.

As DOWNES steps down from the podium and proceeds across the dance floor . . .

The room erupts into a flurry of activity and chatter as PEOPLE make rapid departures or discuss their predicament with one another. A group of AUSTRALIAN SOLDIERS begin to ransack the bar, where a group of CHINESE BARMEN attempt, unsuccessfully, to prevent them. The DANCE BAND packs up, HOTEL STAFF stand around also discussing their next moves—in a variety of languages. In the distance there is the whistle and "crump" of falling shells.

Amid the confusion, ADRIENNE PARGITER and her FRIENDS stand by the edge of the ballroom, stunned. MRS. DICKSON drains her glass. PARGITER puts his arm around his wife, ADRIENNE.

PARGITER
Well. Now we know. They can see—which we were told they couldn't . . . and they can fight—which we were told they couldn't.

ADRIENNE
And they're here—which we were told they'd never be.

The ballroom quickly empties.

EXT. DOCKS. NIGHT.

The scene is one of chaos as thousands of WOMEN and CHILDREN, most of them escorted by their HUSBANDS or MILITARY PERSONNEL, search along the docks for a berth on one of the departing ships.

The ships are virtually all small cargo vessels, not passenger liners. They are mostly devoid of armaments, except for a couple of machine guns mounted on the front decks.

Lighting is kept to a minimum because of the Japanese bombardment. Some of the SHIPS' OFFICERS carry torches, but the ships themselves show nothing more than minimum work lights. Flashes from explosions intermittently illuminate the frantic scene for a few seconds. There is a tremendous amount of noise from vehicles, ships' engines—and PEOPLE—as advice is given and farewells exchanged.

EXT. END OF DOCKS. NIGHT.

Two army trucks arrive. In the driving cabin of the front one are BILL SEARY and two Australian soldiers (EDGAR and PHIL). They stop among a group of cars of all descriptions that have brought the WIVES and CHILDREN of civilian employees to the ships. The cars are being unloaded, CHILDREN are crying, apprehensive WIVES are trying to put on a brave face in front of one another. MALAY PORTERS carry possessions to the ships.

The SOLDIERS leap out of the back of the truck and begin helping a GROUP (25) of uniformed AUSTRALIAN NURSES to clamber out, as well as a couple of AUSTRALIAN WOMEN in army uniform—among them SUSAN, OGGI, EDNA, and BETT. Almost all of the WOMEN are very young—in their mid- to late 20s.

EDGAR
Come on, girlie, just leap into me arms.

He helps one girl to the ground.

EDGAR (to next girl)
That's it, girlie, just leap. . . .

He stops abruptly as a middle-aged matron (MATRON HEFFERNAN) gives him a cold stare. His manner changes as he gingerly takes her arm to help her down.

A blast nearby shakes the area. The SOLDIERS yell for everyone to get down. They all scramble under and around the trucks. The docks shake, debris rains down, the smoke increases. BILL puts his arm protectively around SUSAN.

EXT. SKY. POV. NIGHT.

No planes can be seen, but there are a few flashes in the darkness.

9

EXT. DOCKS. NIGHT.

Another bomb falls, not too far away. The blast rocks the clock tower above the dock.

BILL

Take cover!!!

The tower shakes, then falls, as everyone scrambles to crawl under the army vehicles. The GIRLS all bury their faces in their arms as the debris falls all around. They look up as the blast subsides. EVERYONE is covered in dust. They choke and cough.

BILL

(to Susan) This isn't quite what I'd planned for us.

SUSAN looks toward him, her eyes weeping with the dust.

SUSAN

Oh really.

EXT. ANOTHER PART OF THE DOCK. NIGHT

Among the crowd, ADRIENNE PARGITER moves up the gangplank of the *Prince Albert*. WILLIAM carries a small suitcase for her; he sets it down and looks around. SHIP'S OFFICERS are calling for all nontraveling personnel to leave immediately.

PARGITER

I should've sent you home months ago.

ADRIENNE

At least Charles will be surprised. I wouldn't have seen him until your next leave.

They kiss sedately, both determined to retain their composure. TOPSY passes them, still wearing her dining clothes, but with a coat thrown over the top. She is carrying a small suitcase.

TOPSY

Good evening. Nice night for the collapse of an Empire.

ROSEMARY and DENNIS are embracing by the foot of the gangplank of the small cargo ship *Prince Albert*. WOMEN and CHILDREN are boarding the ship (including MRS. O'RIORDEN and her children, SIOBHAN and ARAN). The SHIP'S CREW are doing their best to get underway, etc. OTHER PEOPLE are walking up and down the dock area searching for available berths. Smoke and darkness add to the confusion.

DENNIS

Come on now . . . before you know it we'll be back in Portsmouth . . . sailing . . . you're a great outdoor girl, Rosemary, that's one thing I love about you.

ROSEMARY

(whispers) And indoors? I thought you liked me indoors? . . .

DENNIS

(embarrassed) Indoors. Oh yes!

The GROUP of 25 AUSTRALIAN NURSES plus FEMALE AUSTRALIAN ARMY PERSONNEL pass them on their way onto the ship. MATRON HEFFERNAN supervises. (The GROUP splits—so that about 15 girls board the *Prince Albert* while others head toward the ships farther down the dock.)

Nearby MRS. ROBERTS is arguing with a jaded ship's officer (LIEUTENANT WESTMACOTT). Her daughter (CELIA) stands nearby, fidgeting with embarrassment. Her husband, ROBBIE ROBERTS, stands dutifully in the background. A huge pile of suitcases is stacked next to a well-kept Bentley.

WESTMACOTT

I'm sorry, madam, but it's only one suitcase each. That dog isn't advisable, either.

MRS. ROBERTS clutches her tiny dog, TILLINGWORTH, even more tightly to her bosom.

MRS. ROBERTS

What rubbish! Are you aware my husband is head of the Singapore PWD?!

CELIA

(embarrassed) Mummy . . .

WESTMACOTT

He could be the King of Bongo Bongo. You can still only take one suitcase on board. Right. That's it. Gangway stowed.

MRS. ROBERTS is willing to continue arguing the point but there is a sudden roar from the engines. SAILORS rapidly begin to untie the mooring ropes and begin to pull up the gangplanks. MRS. ROBERTS and CELIA have no alternative but to hurry on board. ROBBIE ROBERTS turns to the CHINESE DRIVER beside him, who has been helping with the suitcase.

11

ROBBIE

(indicating the car) Take it to the end of the wharf, Chee Wan, and push it off. Damned if I'll have some bloody Japanese officer driving it about.

EXT. DECK OF *PRINCE ALBERT*. NIGHT.

The entire deck of the ship is covered with WOMEN and CHILDREN, packed shoulder to shoulder. MOTHERS cover their CHILDREN with blankets and coats, trying to encourage them to sleep, although most of them are over-excited and enjoying themselves. They run around, giggling and chasing one another. A BOY falls over ROSEMARY. She reaches out a hand to help him. She smiles. Her eyes are wet from tears.

INT. *PRINCE ALBERT* MESS (DINING ROOM). NIGHT.

PASSENGERS, mostly WOMEN and small CHILDREN, but with a few older MEN, are lying all over the floor and tables, trying to make themselves comfortable for the night. Virtually all of the PASSENGERS are middle-class ladies, unused to anything other than first-class travel, but are, for the most part, doing their best to cope. Many of them add a touch of surrealism by being dressed in fashionable evening wear, with elaborate coiffure and jewelry.
Two SEAMEN are distributing life jackets. ADRIENNE PARGITER and MRS. DICKSON and MRS. PIKE—among other well-dressed English ladies—are occupying the crowded and small ship's mess.

SEAMAN FRANCIS

Life jackets on. Do 'em up. Nice 'n' tight. Just ask me if yer don't know how. Be glad to help you, ladies.

MRS. O'RIORDEN

So what's goin' to happen to the men, do you think?

The remark is addressed to no one in particular. MRS. O'RIORDEN is dark, almost gypsy-looking. She has a strong Irish brogue. Her two children, ARAN and SIOBHAN, are beside her.

MRS. PIKE

With us out of the way they're probably already tucked up with their Malayan girlfriends.

She takes a drink from a small flask taken out of her handbag. ADRIENNE glances at her as she drinks.

MRS. O'RIORDEN

It seems so ridiculous. . . . Shovin' us all out at the last minute. . . .

She is busy tying up her children's life jackets as she speaks.

MRS. DICKSON

It seems now they should have shoved us out months ago.

ADRIENNE

In fairness, Phyllis, we could have gone. I think we chose to stay.

She looks up as a mug of tea is offered to her by SUSAN. OGGI and EDNA are also distributing tea to other passengers.

ADRIENNE

Thanks . . . you're all Australians?

SUSAN

That's right. We've been in Singapore for two months.

MRS. DICKSON

And now that they must really need nurses, you're leaving.

ADRIENNE

Phyllis!

SUSAN

Oh, it's true. It's ridiculous.

BETT is sitting nearby. She takes a mug of tea. She is about the same age as the nurse, but is dressed in Australian army uniform.

BETT

I was a secretary at army HQ. I saw the reports on what the Japs did to the nurses in Shanghai and Hong Kong.

SUSAN pauses by a plain, dumpy, middle-aged woman with thick glasses who is praying to herself—MARGARET DRUMMOND. She hesitates to interrupt with the tea. MISS DRUMMOND looks up and takes the mug from her.

MISS DRUMMOND

Oh, oh, don't go, lovely. He can wait. He'll still be there.

EXT. SINGAPORE HARBOR. NIGHT.

The darkened ship moves away from the city, which can be seen in the background, dotted with fires and explosions.

INT. *PRINCE ALBERT* CABIN. NIGHT.

The tiny cabin, with only two bunks, contains seven WOMEN and two SMALL CHILDREN—MRS. ROBERTS and her daughter, CELIA; TOPSY MERRITT; MRS. TIPPLER and her two sons, DANNY and MICHAEL; and two English schoolteachers, BEATRICE and MAVIS. MRS. ROBERTS sits uncomfortably in a chair, struggling with her life jacket. She can't make head or tail of the strings. Her daughter, CELIA, demonstrates with her own jacket.

                        CELIA
It's really quite simple, Mummy. Look. Like this.

TOPSY MERRITT, still in the satin dress she was wearing at Raffles, watches MRS. ROBERTS continue to struggle with the cords. She reaches across and takes them.

                        TOPSY
Here. Let me do it.

                   MRS. ROBERTS
Thank you. *(recognizing her)* Oh, Mrs. . . .

                        TOPSY
Merritt. Topsy Merritt.

                   MRS. ROBERTS
Of course. The American. Your husband runs the pineapple canning factory.

                        TOPSY
Right. He's the top dog in pineapples.

She struggles with the strings on the life vest. MRS. ROBERTS looks around the absurdly overcrowded cabin. The TWO BOYS are arguing over possession of a toy car. MRS. ROBERTS appeals to their MOTHER.

                   MRS. ROBERTS
Perhaps the boys could be restrained a little? I realize conditions are somewhat . . . unusual . . . but this *is my* cabin. . . .

14

MRS. TIPPLER

Your cabin! *My* cabin! *(She is confrontational, assertive. She speaks with a flat London accent.)*

TOPSY

I understood Marty had arranged this cabin for me.

MRS. TIPPLER

My husband is an engineer with Coastal Traders.

MRS. ROBERTS

Mine is head of the PWD!

TOPSY

Mine's in pineapples. Look, girls . . . we're just gonna have to get along. It's only for five weeks.

MRS. ROBERTS rolls her eyes at the thought. MRS. TIPPLER glowers.

EXT. *PRINCE ALBERT*. DAY.

Under a hot tropical sun the ship proceeds down the Malacca Straits, within sight of land. The sea is calm, glassy.

EXT. DECK OF *PRINCE ALBERT*. DAY.

The heat is unbearable and the PASSENGERS have done their best to find some shade by rigging blankets and coats.

INT. SHIP'S PASSAGEWAY. DAY

SUSAN, EDNA, OGGI, and SEAMAN FRANCIS, carrying soup vats, are squeezing past WESTMACOTT, who is enjoying their proximity.

SUSAN

How much longer do we have to wear these?

She indicates the life vests. FRANCIS glances at his watch.

SEAMAN FRANCIS

Should be okay about now. Eleven hours out of Singapore and we're out of range of the Jap fighters.

EXT. SHIP'S DECK. DAY.

MISS DRUMMOND

But now the goddess Hera, the wicked stepmother, was so jealous of Hercules that one night she crept into his room and put two deadly snakes in his cradle . . . but he was . . .

She breaks off abruptly as the ship's siren begins to sound.

EXT. SKY. DAY.

A group of six Japanese fighter planes come hurtling out of the sun toward the *Prince Albert*. They begin to drop their bombs. Huge sprays of water surge into the air like geysers close to the ship.

INT. *PRINCE ALBERT* PASSAGEWAY. DAY.

The ship rocks violently as a near-miss hits the water a few feet from the port side. SUSAN, EDNA, SEAMAN FRANCIS, and OGGI drop soup vats as they stagger from one side of the passageway to the other.

INT. *PRINCE ALBERT*. CABIN. DAY.

The ship lurches with the force of the near-miss and water bursts in through the porthole, drenching MRS. ROBERTS, who leaps to her feet, screaming. TILLINGWORTH begins to bark angrily.

EXT. *PRINCE ALBERT* DECK. DAY.

PASSENGERS throw themselves flat on the deck and cling to anything stable as the ship begins zigzagging to dodge the Japanese fighters.

MONTAGE SEQUENCE:

During the bombardment, a group of Japanese planes attack the ship . . .
planes wheel and turn . . .
PILOTS aim . . .
the ship's wheel spins . . .
rudder alters course . . .
bombs hit the water on either side of the vessel . . .
PEOPLE on deck and below deck anxiously but fairly calmly wait for either a bomb to hit or the planes to depart. . . .
MISS DRUMMOND has her arms around a GROUP of CHILDREN. . . .

INT. *PRINCE ALBERT* BRIDGE. DAY.

The wheel spins furiously. The ship lists to one side, then CAPTAIN MUR-CHISON and other OFFICERS grab it and spin it back again.

Another bomb sends spray up over the ship in a near-miss.

The bridge is then totally demolished by a direct hit.

SAILOR

Abandon ship!

INT. *PRINCE ALBERT* CABIN/PASSAGEWAY. DAY.

The ship is listing, water is ankle-deep in the galleyway and cabin. A SEA-MAN is helping the WOMEN and CHILDREN, who are moving toward the stairway leading to the deck.

MRS. ROBERTS has trouble fitting her bulk, increased by the life jacket, through the doorway. She is still clutching her DOG, who is yelping furiously. CELIA pulls on one side of her, TOPSY pushes on the other.

CELIA

Turn sideways, Mummy, sideways!

SAILOR

(helping push) I don't reckon she's got a sideways.

With an effort MRS. ROBERTS moves from the doorway into the corridor. She is pushed along toward the stairs, still protesting.

Part of the bridge falls onto the main deck among the passengers, killing a number of them in the process. A siren begins wailing loudly, SAILORS grab the cork life rafts and begin throwing them over the side of the ship, into the water.

The planes continue bombing the ship. One of them advances menacingly across the water and begins to fire its machine guns. EVERYONE on deck rapidly lies flat. ADRIENNE PARGITER shields a CHILD with her body as bullets hit all around.

INT. *PRINCE ALBERT* DINING ROOM. DAY.

SAILORS and OFFICERS are shepherding the PASSENGERS toward the exits. The CROWD is surprisingly orderly despite the water, smoke, tilting ship, and the sound of bombs and machine guns. The AUSTRALIAN NURSES calmly help with the organization. TOPSY angrily pulls up her dress after someone steps on it.

A second hit, somewhere astern, rocks the vessel. Smoke billows into the dining room from the passageways.

EXT. DECK OF *PRINCE ALBERT*. DAY.

MISS DRUMMOND is herding the children toward the ship's railing. The deck of the ship is now on fire in three or four places. Many dead lie around, others are wounded; there is smoke and flame, the roar of bombs, the chatter of machine guns.

MICHAEL
(to Miss Drummond) Are we sinking?

MISS DRUMMOND
That's right, dear. We're going to jump into the water. It's going to be lovely.

He grins.

EXT. *PRINCE ALBERT* DECK. DAY.

ADRIENNE PARGITER gets up; she tries to rouse the CHILD she sheltered, then realizes he's dead.

The SAILORS are helping people over the railing so they can jump into the sea. An attacking Japanese plane, now out of bombs, returns suddenly and opens fire along the deck with its machine guns. The SAILORS, PASSENGERS, and NURSES (who have been helping getting everyone off the deck) dive for cover.

When the plane has passed they get up again, although a number remain dead on the deck, among them FIVE of the AUSTRALIAN NURSES. SUSAN gets to her feet, then looks around for MATRON HEFFERNAN. She sees her lying by the ship's railing, dead. She stares for a moment, disbelieving.

The OTHERS pause for a moment, still stunned by the death of the MATRON, whose body is lying sprawled a few feet away, riddled with bullets. Then THEY turn and proceed to carry out Susan's instructions.

ADRIENNE PARGITER looks around for her friends, MRS. PIKE and MRS. DICKSON, but can't see them among the smoke and confusion. She jumps from the railing into the water and begins to swim away from the sinking ship.

MRS. ROBERTS emerges onto the deck, which is now on a marked slant. TOPSY and CELIA help her across the BODIES and debris toward one of the railings. The lifeboats are all being lowered to the water. Some are already in the sea and, heavily overloaded, are pulling away from the ship.

> ### CELIA
> We'll have to jump, Mummy!

MRS. ROBERTS looks down—the debris-strewn sea, the waves crashing against the ship, oil, bodies, etc.

> ### MRS. ROBERTS
> No thank you, dear. I'll stay here.

> ### TOPSY
> The ship is sinking, Mrs. Roberts!

ROSEMARY LEIGHTON-JONES approaches them. She sees the drama with MRS. ROBERTS.

> ### ROSEMARY
> Hullo, Mrs. Roberts. Remember me? . . .

MRS. ROBERTS looks blank. It's all too much for her.

> ### ROSEMARY
> . . . Rosemary Leighton-Jones. We met at the cricket club. My husband was captain of the first eleven . . .

> ### MRS. ROBERTS
> Oh, of course, dear. How are you?

> ### ROSEMARY
> Very well, thank you. . . .

> ### TOPSY
> Some other time, maybe.

ROSEMARY

Yes. Just take my hand, Mrs. Roberts, we'll jump together.

MRS. ROBERTS

Of course.

She takes the older lady's hand. They jump into the sea, MRS. ROBERTS still clutching her DOG. TOPSY and CELIA follow.

EXT. SEA BY THE *PRINCE ALBERT*. DAY.

PEOPLE are thrashing around in the water. Some are on the life rafts, helping pull others up onto the surface. Some rafts are already low in the water from their load of people. Some PASSENGERS are swimming as quickly as they can away from the sinking ship. A number of BODIES float in the water, which is strewn with debris. Heavy smoke drifts across the scene, causing further confusion.

SUSAN looks around for some sign of her friends. She sees no one, looks toward the ship, then begins to swim away from it.

The Japanese planes, now out of ammunition, have gone.

EXT. OPEN SEA. DAY.

It is late afternoon. All the noise has ceased. No screams, bombs or guns. No people. Just the swell of the sea and, in the distance, a coastline.

SUSAN drifts into the shot, clinging to some wreckage from the *Prince Albert*. After a few seconds, ADRIENNE PARGITER appears over a swell, also clinging to wreckage.

SUSAN

It could be worse, I suppose.

ADRIENNE

Do you think so?

SUSAN

The water could be cold.

ADRIENNE

That's true.

They lift with a wave, then, as they float down the other side, ROSEMARY LEIGHTON-JONES is revealed. All three are bedraggled from the sea and exposure, with their clothes tattered and burnt from the explosions and fires on the ship.

SUSAN

Must be Sumatra.

ROSEMARY

Yes.

SUSAN

Amazing how everyone's just . . . disappeared.

ROSEMARY

It's like one of those girl's Adventure Annuals my mother gave me every Christmas.

ADRIENNE

It's an adventure I could do without.

ROSEMARY

Oh . . . they always had happy endings.

EXT. SEA. NIGHT

SUSAN, ADRIENNE, and ROSEMARY are still paddling toward the shore, which can be seen quite clearly in the bright moonlight. It is considerably closer.

SUSAN

Now I'm cold.

ROSEMARY

If you spend a penny it'll warm you up.

SUSAN and ADRIENNE both look at her quizzically.

ROSEMARY

We used to swim in the North Sea in our school hols. It was freezing. We always did it.

There is a moment's silence.

SUSAN

Mmmmmm . . . it's working . . .

The three women laugh.

EXT. SHORE. EARLY MORNING.

Not a tropical beach but a mangrove swamp, muddy, with dense undergrowth, crabs and snakes. Exhausted, bedraggled, with torn clothes and skin black from oil and fire, SUSAN, ADRIENNE, and ROSEMARY crawl from the sea.

They sink into the mud. Each step becomes an effort, but they push their way through the low bushes and vines, which scratch them and tear their clothes.

They freeze as they see two large crocodiles in the mud a short distance away. The crocodiles lazily amble away from them.

They continue as fast as possible through the slime.

Finally they collapse on a small piece of drier ground. No one else is in sight. There is no sound but the breaking of waves on the shore.

ROSEMARY

I'm starving.

ADRIENNE AND SUSAN

Me, too.

They all smile, weakly. ROSEMARY turns and looks at the others.

ROSEMARY

Rosemary Leighton-Jones. My husband is Dennis Leighton-Jones, Royal Malayan Volunteers.

SUSAN

Susan Macarthy. Australian Nursing Corps.

ADRIENNE

Adrienne Pargiter. Wife of tea planter.

ADRIENNE's introduction has a slight touch of irony.

ROSEMARY

How do you do.

EXT. ROAD. DAY.

It is sometime in the early afternoon. The sun is high. The shadows are almost directly underneath. SUSAN, ADRIENNE, and ROSEMARY walk slowly along a narrow dirt road. Dense forest is on one side and rice fields on the other, but there is no sign of life.

ADRIENNE is the first to notice an odd, rhythmic, metallic sound. She looks around and sees nothing. The others hear the noise and also turn to look. Slowly, a MAN appears on a bicycle, then another, then another. An endless row of MEN on bicycles. As they come closer they are identifiable as JAPANESE SOLDIERS, all with rifles slung across their backs. The three WOMEN watch. They move to one side to let the procession pass, though it seems never-ending. None of the CYCLISTS pays the slightest attention to the WOMEN.

Among the CYCLISTS appears a 1938 Dodge, in excellent condition. It is overtaking the cyclists, but stops when it reaches the three WOMEN. The occupants are a CHAUFFEUR, in army uniform, and a JAPANESE OFFICER. (This is CAPTAIN TANAKA). The OFFICER gestures. The WOMEN pause a moment, then get into the car. He snaps an order in Japanese and it moves off again.

INT. CAR. DAY.

The OFFICER turns to look at the WOMEN. He is immaculately dressed, in a tailored uniform (unlike that of any Japanese officers or soldiers seen subsequently). He is good-looking, with a small mustache. A white silk scarf is around his neck, adorned with the "Rising Sun" emblem.

TANAKA

You are English ladies?

He speaks excellent English with a slight American accent.

ADRIENNE AND ROSEMARY

Yes.

SUSAN

Australian.

TANAKA

Ahh . . . yes . . . I was for some years in Singapore. I was a . . . newspaper correspondent . . . May I ask what you ladies are doing here in Sumatra?

The three WOMEN exchange a glance.

ADRIENNE

Our ship was sunk.

SUSAN

By your planes.

ROSEMARY

We swam to shore.

TANAKA

What can I say? Except that attacking the enemy is a . . . characteristic of war.

ADRIENNE

The *Prince Albert* was full of women and children, not soldiers.

TANAKA

A matter of regret.

ADRIENNE

More than that. There's a Geneva Convention laying down the rules of war . . .

TANAKA

(sharply) Japan has signed no Geneva Convention. If war has begun it can only mean the time for rules has ended. The aim is to win . . .

He turns and looks ahead, along the road. The WOMEN exchange uneasy glances.

EXT. PALEMBANG. DAY.

The car stops in a narrow, cluttered street of a provincial town. The DRIVER gets out and opens the door. The OFFICER watches the THREE WOMEN as they leave the car.

TANAKA

Hache Doro. Good luck.

He gestures immediately to the DRIVER. The car leaves.

ROSEMARY
(to Adrienne) Up until you reminded him about the Geneva Convention I thought we were going to be invited to dine.

She is suddenly clouted, hard, across the head by a stockily built Japanese soldier who hisses (as a way of getting attention) before he speaks. This is THE SNAKE.

THE SNAKE
Ssssss. Boloh! Buggero! Speedo! Speedo!

He roughly pushes all three of them down the laneway, which opens into a large square, flanked on each side by ornate Chinese temples. The square is packed with EUROPEANS who have made it ashore from the sunken ships. They are being herded into lines, MEN and WOMEN separately (there are far more WOMEN and CHILDREN than MEN) by JAPANESE SOLDIERS. There is a tremendous amount of noise and confusion.

On spikes around the perimeter of the square are a number of severed heads—of ASIAN MEN. ADRIENNE, ROSEMARY, and SUSAN notice them with revulsion.

They look among the CROWD for familiar faces. There are a number of people from the *Prince Albert*, all in poor condition—torn clothes, dirty and badly sunburnt. In addition, many are bloody from wounds, some have broken limbs.

Among the GROUP, MRS. ROBERTS and her daughter CELIA; MRS. TIPPLER and her two SONS; TOPSY MERRITT; MRS. O'RIORDEN and her two CHILDREN; MISS DRUMMOND; MRS. DICKSON; MRS. PIKE; DR. VERSTAK; MICHELE RUETTE, etc. SUSAN sees a group of SIX AUSTRALIAN NURSES, including OGGI and EDNA, also BETT, whose army uniform is now in shreds. She manages to slip in beside them. She looks around.

SUSAN

How'd you get here?

OGGI

Jap navy boat picked us up.

SUSAN

What were they like?

EDNA

Gentlemen—compared with this lot.

SUSAN looks around the vast crowd.

THE SNAKE

English empire number ten. Nippon soldier number one.

EXT. COUNTRY ROAD. LATE AFTERNOON.

The sun is lower but the heat and humidity are still excessive. The faces of the now totally exhausted WOMEN are dripping with sweat.

EXT. CAMP. LATE AFTERNOON.

The WOMEN pass through a pair of roughly built gates, crisscrossed with barbed wire. The barbed wire continues on a hastily built fence that surrounds the entire camp. On the far side is a large house built in impressive Dutch colonial style—double storied with a large columned verandah on the ground floor.

They cross a dusty compound toward a group of thatched huts probably built to house estate workers. The huts are in two rows. One of the rows is already occupied—a number of WOMEN and CHILDREN, mostly well built and fair-haired, watch the new arrivals. (These are the LOCAL EUROPEAN INHABITANTS—all Dutch.) There is also a GROUP of DUTCH NUNS, all in immaculate habits. Their ages vary from early 20s into the 50s. The head nun, a tall, striking-looking woman of 35, is SISTER WILHELMINA.

EXT. CAMP. NIGHT.

The rows of huts are dark and silent. The lighting around the camp is eccentric, with a few low wattage bulbs placed at irregular intervals around the huts. The wire fence surrounding the camp is lit more brilliantly, but unevenly.

A COUPLE of JAPANESE GUARDS stand casually near the main gate, smoking and talking.

The sound of night birds, frogs, and insects is fairly loud from the forest beyond the camp.

INT. HUT. NIGHT.

Although hot, cramped and uncomfortable, almost everyone is asleep. SUSAN lies awake. Numerous mosquitoes buzz around. Cockroaches emerge from the walls and scuttle around the sleepers.

EXT. HUTS. EARLY MORNING.

A GROUP of JAPANESE GUARDS run at high speed up and down the huts banging the side with sticks and yelling ''Tenko, Tenko'' and ''Speedo, speedo'' at the tops of their voices.

(These guards become familiar as the story progresses. They are known by nicknames . . . ''THE SNAKE''—the head guard, very aggressive and powerfully built, whose instructions are all preceded by a hiss, to get attention; ''LOFTY''—a tall for a Japanese young guard who finds it difficult to be aggressive toward the women; "MR. MOTO"—a guard who resembles a popular detective; "BORIS"—who bears some resemblance to Boris Karloff; "RAGS"—a young man who habitually wears a hopscotch of clothes.)

INT. BRITISH HUT. EARLY MORNING.

The WOMEN are astonished at the racket and look around, puzzled. The JAPANESE burst into the huts, continuing their yelling. They push the WOMEN toward the outside, slapping and kicking them with abandon. A few WOMEN try to ask THE SNAKE what is happening. His only reply is to scream "boloh" and "buggero" and bash them hard across the face.

EXT. COMPOUND. EARLY MORNING.

The WOMEN are roughly pushed into lines by the JAPANESE GUARDS, who are yelling so loudly and repeatedly it is impossible for any questions to be asked. Anyone who speaks is instantly slapped hard across the face. Many are in tears from the treatment. SUSAN, ROSEMARY and ADRIENNE comfort some of those crying. Only the CHILDREN are never touched and look around at the proceedings with fascination.

The gates open and a JAPANESE OFFICER enters, sword at his side. He is accompanied by two smartly dressed GUARDS and an apprehensive-looking INTERPRETER.

The GUARDS carry a table, which is placed in front of the assembled WOMEN. Among them are two tiny Chinese women, WING and MILLIE. Wing is 44, MILLIE is of indeterminate age.

The officer (COLONEL HIROTA) is in his mid-to late 30s. His uniform is clean and pressed but has seen much better days. He speaks in Japanese. THE INTERPRETER listens nervously. HIROTA pauses. THE INTERPRETER is unsure if he wants him to begin translating or not, so does nothing. HIROTA snaps something at him.

INTERPRETER
I am Colonel Hirota and I am . . . in charge of these . . . this place. . . . Days of British and Dutch people exploiting Oriental people all finish. . . .

WING
(whispering) Now *they* exploit Oriental peoples.

INTERPRETER
In the past you Europeans had great proudery and arrogance. Think Oriental people inferior. Situation now 100% reverse.

COLONEL HIROTA begins to speak again, but MRS. DICKSON raises her hand, then begins to talk. The JAPANESE look toward her, shocked momentarily into immobility.

29

MRS. DICKSON

Colonel, I would like to know how long you expect us to remain in these perfectly appalling conditions.

She is interrupted by the sudden arrival of THE SNAKE, who hits her so hard across the face she flies backward through the rank of WOMEN behind her and falls to the ground, her lip bleeding profusely. Some WOMEN go to help her.

THE SNAKE

No!

They stop, look at him, and resume their places. MARGARET DRUMMOND pauses, then kneels beside MRS. DICKSON. She lifts her head from the ground and dabs at her bloody mouth with the sleeve of her dress. THE SNAKE looks as if he is about to walk to her and strike her, but is stopped by a glance from COLONEL HIROTA.

Outside the gate, RAGS, at a signal from COLONEL HIROTA, gingerly puts a needle onto a 78 rpm record on an old phonograph, which is hooked up to a speaker above the gate.

Following an order from the OFFICER, the JAPANESE SOLDIERS begin yelling "Keirei, keirei." No one understands what this means. Immediately, the JAPANESE leap among the CROWD; slapping and punching indiscriminately (although they don't touch the CHILDREN), continuing to yell "Keirei, keirei."

"Bow," someone calls out, "it means bow." The word runs up and down the lines. Slowly, the WOMEN and CHILDREN begin bowing. If the bows aren't low enough, or too tentative, the JAPANESE slap then again, yelling, "Keirei!"

Finally, all the PRISONERS are bowing low toward the flag, with its Rising Sun emblem, fluttering high over the camp. The JAPANESE OFFICERS remain saluting, the SOLDIERS bow.

A scratchy version of the Japanese national anthem begins. The JAPANESE face their flag and salute.

EXT. COMPOUND. DAY.

A large amount of meat, mostly offal and fat, is dumped onto the dirt. Rice and vegetables are dropped beside it.

The truck that dumped the food drives off through the gates. The GUARDS watch, amused for the most part, as the WOMEN attempt to gather up the food in a variety of inadequate containers.

SISTER WILHELMINA

Take it all to the kitchen. Please bring everything to the kitchen.

INT. BRITISH HUT. NIGHT. DAY.

Inside the hut, the food is being doled out of buckets by DUTCH NUNS and a few other BRITISH and DUTCH WOMEN. The portions are tiny and the food looks unappetizing. There is a mixture of crockery and cutlery. Some are eating off pieces of wood and some are using Chinese-style chopsticks.

It is hot and humid. Insects cluster around the one low-wattage light bulb over a doorway.

There is a silence as everyone picks at the food, their hunger tending to overcome their distaste. The national anthem fades away.

> ROSEMARY
>
> This isn't so bad really.

A number of incredulous looks follow this remark.

> ROSEMARY
>
> Well . . . I went to an English boarding school. I meant by those standards.

MRS. TIPPLER looks at the tiny amount of food on her plate.

> MRS. TIPPLER
>
> It's funny . . . in the kitchen there seemed so *much*.

> MRS. DICKSON
>
> What do you mean?

> MRS. TIPPLER
>
> Well . . . How do we know they're dividing it up fairly . . . the Dutch . . .

She is "shushed" by some who point to the DUTCH NUNS still doling out food at the other end of the hut.

> MRS. TIPPLER
>
> They don't speak English.

> ADRIENNE
>
> The food you saw was divided up among over 400 people.

One of the Dutch nuns, the young and attractive SISTER ANNA, passes back through the GROUP.

SISTER ANNA

That's correct. It doesn't go far.

She smiles and gives no indication of being offended. Her English is almost accentless. MRS. PIKE glares after her.

MRS. PIKE

I don't know that the Dutch are noted for their cooking. . . .

Her comment is offered in a prim, tentative manner.
HELEN, the young Dutch girl who has been helping the NUNS dole out food, turns to MRS. PIKE.

HELEN

No. Nod like de English people.

MRS. DICKSON touches her swollen lip.

MRS. DICKSON

All I can say is I hope this is over very, very soon.

TOPSY

When our boys get here it'll be just a few weeks.

OGGI

Your boys? What about *our* boys? They'll be the ones. . . .

MRS. PIKE

Frankly, I don't care which boys do it. Just as long as we're going home.

BETT

(*to Oggi*) She's right. Any boys'll do me.

OGGI

Thought they might.

MRS. O'RIORDEN stands and speaks as if imparting vital information.

MRS. O'RIORDEN

I've heard they're sending all the noncombatants home. What do you think about that now?

There is silence for a moment. Some are skeptical about the information. Others want to believe it's true.

DR. VERSTAK

Vere you did hear that?

MRS. O'RIORDEN

Oh, just around and about. One of the . . .

ADRIENNE

(*overlapping*) We're *all* noncombatants, Mrs. O'Riorden. . . .

MRS. O'RIORDEN

No. I mean like me. I'm Irish an' we're neutral an' there's . . . two Portuguese ladies an' (she looks around to Dr. Verstak) . . . an' you, you're . . .

DR. VERSTAK

I haff a German passport.

MRS. O'RIORDEN

Well then, you're on their side, aren't you?

DR. VERSTAK

So you think? Already I have escape two madmen in Europe. Now I am catch by ze Oriental version.

ADRIENNE leans across to her.

ADRIENNE

You were in Singapore? I don't think we met. . . .

DR. VERSTAK

I don't think. The English don't invite Jewish refugees to ze cricket club. Yes. My husband and me, we are doctors in Asian hospital.

SUSAN

You're a doctor?

DR. VERSTAK

That is vot I say. You like perhaps I send to Leipzig for ze certificate?

SUSAN

Oh, no. I . . .

MRS. TIPPLER

Anyway, they're sure to let you go.

WING

No. Japanese man (*she pronounces it* "maren") doan like lady. Call Japanese lady "zashiki buta." Means "old pig in back of house."

WING speaks without the benefit of commas or full stops, though she is quite easily understood. MRS. ROBERTS looks up sharply as WING speaks, rather surprised and a little offended at her breezy participation in the conversation.

MRS. PIKE

(*to herself*) Sounds strangely familiar. . . .

MISS DRUMMOND

I was in China when the Japanese invaded. I think the people they despised most were Europeans . . . then prisoners . . . then women.

ADRIENNE

Well. That's us. All three.

EXT. RICE PADDIES. DAY.

A GROUP of WOMEN are working in the fields, knee-deep in water, under a blazing sun. A closer shot reveals them to be WOMEN from the camp. Their clothes are battered and often improvised from bits and pieces. They wear a variety of hats, including the traditional conical "coolie" hat, as protection against the sun.

The women include MRS. PIKE, ADRIENNE, TOPSY.

TWO GUARDS are at the end of the paddy, sitting under a palm tree, their rifles propped casually beside them. One is "MR. MOTO" and the other is "RAGS."

EXT. FOREST. DAY.

Another GROUP of WOMEN, including MISS DRUMMOND, EDNA, SISTER ANNA, two other NUNS, and MILLIE are gathering firewood, which is being cut from trees with small blunt axes. They stagger along the forest paths under heavy loads. GUARDS casually watch them, doing nothing to help.

EXT. STREAM. DAY.

Another GROUP, including CELIA ROBERTS, WING, and MICHELE, are collecting water in buckets from a small stream. The buckets are scooped in the water, then passed up the bank in a chain. At the top, on the pathway, they are hooked onto each end of a pole, then lifted and carried off in the direction of the camp. The buckets are heavy and the WOMEN stagger under the weight.

MICHELE

(*calling to guard*) Yasume?

GUARD

Yasume nei. Yasume nei.

He gestures forcefully along the direction of the path. A rest denied, the WOMEN lift their loads and continue.

After some moments, WING turns and looks back at the TWO GUARDS. Both are some distance away, lighting cigarettes. They don't look toward the WOMEN, who make slow progress because of their heavy loads.

She puts her buckets down, then quickly squats over one of them and urinates into it. The others watch, then MICHELE does the same. She gestures to CELIA.

MICHELE

Come . . .

CELIA is embarrassed. She blushes, looks back toward the JAPANESE, then squats over her bucket.

INT/EXT. KITCHEN. DAY.

Under the supervision of SISTER WILHELMINA food is being prepared. A NUN is picking maggots out of the offal. THE SNAKE ambles into the area and looks around. The WOMEN bow to him.

In the background, a group of CHILDREN are playing "countries," i.e., one child throws the ball into the air and calls the name of a country. The other kids run; the one who is the country named has to retrieve the ball. He/she then calls out "stop," etc.

INT. JAPANESE HUT. DAY.

The inside of the hut is revealed to be the Japanese soldiers' bath house. The atmosphere is steamy. Huge tin baths, each capable of holding 6 MEN, are set up with fires underneath for heating the water. JAPANESE SOLDIERS, clad only in scanty loincloths, are standing by, waiting for water to be added.

As the exhausted WOMEN pour their buckets into the baths, SOLDIERS casually take off their loincloths and climb in. CELIA looks away in embarrassment. MICHELE smiles as she adds her bucket to a bathtub. WING and CELIA add their buckets to the same tub. MICHELE smiles as she sees THE SNAKE come to the doorway, dip a beaker into one of the buckets and drink.

MICHELE

Wiz luck I'ave somesing zey catch.

As they leave WING glances toward MICHELE.

35

WING

(*To Celia*) You see man before.

CELIA

Well. No . . . only here.

WING

Oh. So. Some little Oriental man big like this (*She draws her hands far apart*) an' some big European man like this (*she puts her hands close together*). You nevah can tell. . . .

WING shakes her head in wondrous contemplation.

CELIA

(*further embarrassed*) Really . . .

INT/EXT. LATRINES. DAY.

ROSEMARY, the two Dutch sisters, HELEN (19) and ANTOINETTE (15), as well as BETT and MRS. CRONJE (a non–English-speaking Dutchwoman) are cleaning out the toilet. They are all soaked with sweat, which gleams on their faces, runs in rivulets from their hair and soaks their backs so that their odd assortment of dresses and shirts are pasted to their bodies.

The toilet consists of a long trough cut into the ground, which is used by simply standing astride. ROSEMARY and HELEN are cleaning out the effluent by scooping it up into a coconut shell and emptying the contents into rusty and leaking buckets. The others take their place as they leave with full containers. BETT slips as she steps forward and falls toward the sewer, her face landing almost level with it.

BETT

Bugger!!!

She lifts herself up onto her knees and, very unwillingly, begins bailing into a bucket held by MRS. CRONJE.

BETT

And I thought being a secretary was a rotten job. What if they do win the bloody war?! They'll have us doing this forever!

ROSEMARY

They aren't going to win. We'll win. The British don't lose wars.

BETT

Yeah? I reckon if I'd paid attention at the school I could think of a few. . . .

36

ROSEMARY, HELEN, and ANTOINETTE carefully carry their full buckets outside the latrine area, toward a garden that has been planted behind the huts.

HELEN leaves her SISTER and catches up with ROSEMARY. HELEN is not unattractive, but big and awkward.

HELEN

Dey tell me you are a model.

ROSEMARY

Oh, yes. It's true.

HELEN

I think so. You are very beautiful. You have been to Paris?

ROSEMARY

Many times.

HELEN

(*overawed*) Oh . . . de wonderful clothe, de lovely people, de elegance, oh. . . .

ROSEMARY, covered in sweat and grime, begins to pour the contents of her bucket along the fledgling plants. Some of it splashes onto her legs.

HELEN

In Singapore you model?

ROSEMARY smiles.

ROSEMARY

No. I was visiting my husband there . . . I'm modeling next season for Hartnell's in London . . . well . . . I hope I am.

A gesture with her hand takes in the prison camp. In the background, on the other side of the wire fence surrounding the camp, the WOMEN can be seen who collected water and wood. They are walking toward the Japanese guards' huts.

EXT/INT. BRITISH HUT. LATE AFTERNOON.

The returning WORK PARTIES enter the hut and flop down, exhausted. These include ADRIENNE; MRS. PIKE; MISS DRUMMOND; CELIA; MICHELE; ROSEMARY; EDNA; TOPSY; MRS. DICKSON, etc. (They don't all arrive at once but drift in sporadically.)

MRS. TIPPLER is lying on her mat fanning herself with a palm frond. A few other older WOMEN are also lying around, including MRS. ROBERTS.

ADRIENNE

(*to Mrs. Tippler*) You could do some work.

MRS. TIPPLER

In this heat?!

ADRIENNE

We're all supposed to work if we're not sick. You're just lazy.

MRS. TIPPLER, without moving her body, tips her head toward ADRIENNE.

MRS. TIPPLER

Lazy! Me?!

ADRIENNE

You.

MRS. TIPPLER snorts and resumes fanning herself.

MRS. DICKSON has thrown herself down onto her mat. She is covered in sweat and mud. She is totally exhausted.

MRS. DICKSON

I am completely . . . buggered.

MRS. PIKE

Phyllis!

MRS. DICKSON

I'm sorry. There just is no other word. I am . . . buggered.

MRS. ROBERTS

We can't cope with this. None of us. It's utterly . . . unendurable.

There is a murmur of agreement from all those returning, exhausted, from their various labors. MISS DRUMMOND listens with interest; then she speaks quietly.

MISS DRUMMOND

But . . . just because it's unendurable doesn't mean we can't endure it. We must. The Japanese want to break our spirit. We have to show them who and what we are.

ADRIENNE looks toward MISS DRUMMOND. Her words stop the flow of grumbles.

As they talk, TOPSY moves toward the side of the hut and looks out toward the ramshackle barbed wire fence and the jungle beyond.

TOPSY

You know, this place sure ain't Alcatraz. We could be under that fence and into that jungle before you could say boo.

ADRIENNE

Don't forget to write.

MRS. O'RIORDEN

But you'll die in that jungle. Full of snakes it is. Boa constrictors. Ugh. . . .

TOPSY

Yeah? After three months of this place that doesn't sound so bad.

ADRIENNE

The locals will betray you. The Japanese have got them all terrified.

MRS. O'RIORDEN

That's right. Some of the men escaped and they brought 'em back an' cut off their noses an' ears an' hung them upside down so they did.

This remark is greeted by a mixture of horror and incredulity.

MISS DRUMMOND

Awful! All the loose change would've fallen out of their pockets. They'd have hated that.

MRS. O'RIORDEN

But it's true!

TOPSY slumps toward her mat and flops down onto it.

TOPSY

Well, yeah, you've convinced me it ain't so lousy here. . . . Room service is a bit slow. . . .

ROSEMARY has entered the hut and overhears part of the conversation.

ROSEMARY

What men, Mrs. O'Riorden?

MRS. O'RIORDEN

That guard . . . the one who looks like the actor. . . . you know in all them Japanese detective fillums. . . .

ROSEMARY

Mr. Moto . . . Peter Lorre. Yes, Mrs. O'Riorden . . . but . . . *what men?*

MRS. O'RIORDEN
I'm tellin' you . . . that guard was sayin' . . . there's a camp full of
men . . . just a few miles away. Dutchmen, I'm thinkin', but he says
some's from Singapore.

ROSEMARY looks out of the window toward the jungle on the far side of
the camp.

EXT. HOSPITAL BUILDING. LATE AFTERNOON.

The camp hospital is simply one of the thatched huts, virtually identical to
the prisoners' quarters. It is separated from the other huts, although it, too,
was originally built for estate workers. TWO JAPANESE are walking toward
the building—the INTERPRETER and DR. MIZUSHIMA.

INT. HOSPITAL BUILDING. LATE AFTERNOON.

The interior of the hospital is crowded (though not jammed), mostly with
older WOMEN, lying side by side on the floor, on either straw mats (tatami)
or hessian bags stuffed with straw. No medical equipment is in evidence.
Most of the patients are lying quietly, obviously very ill, but some are feverish
with malaria. (Nursing care is provided by the THREE AUSTRALIAN
NURSES, a few NURSES FROM THE BRITISH GROUP, some of the DUTCH
NUNS, and a few of the ASIANS).
   The TWO JAPANESE enter the building and are immediately confronted
by DR. VERSTAK.

DR. VERSTAK
Hey, Dr. Mizushima-san . . . you get me some quinine, eh? And
some bandages, and morphine. And a stethoscope. Even some as-
pirin is good.

DR. MIZUSHIMA
You want . . .

DR. VERSTAK
Mercurochrome! I know. You Japanese must think it cures everysing. Zen you give me some cigarettes, eh? I'm a German, your ally,
not one of these British colonialists.

She taps DR. MIZUSHIMA'S top pocket. He reluctantly takes the pack out
and offers her one, but she takes the whole pack and slips it into her dress
pocket.

Only Japanese?! Tastes like cow dung.

Some distance away, halfway down the hut, SUSAN and OGGI are dealing with patients. SUSAN is trying to get an elderly woman to drink some soup. She is not very successful. OGGI is tending MRS. VAN PRAAGH (the mother of Helen and Antoinette) across the hut. EDNA is farther down the hut.

DR. VERSTAK walks along the ward. SUSAN stands.

DR. VERSTAK
How she is?

Her question is straightforward, without a personal edge. She is casual but assured. She is puffing on one of the cigarettes she just acquired from DR. MIZUSHIMA.

SUSAN
Oh, doctor. I can't get her to eat anything. I think it's just . . . all too much for her, really. For a lot of them.

SUSAN looks around the room.

DR. VERSTAK
Zey don't adjust, they die, my dear. How many gone since ve come to zis so wonderful place?

OGGI
Four.

DR. VERSTAK
Not so bad. *(she shrugs)* Be vorse by Christmas; wiz so bad food and no medicine.

EDNA is attending a patient across the aisle.

EDNA
Christmas! The war'll be over by Christmas!

DR. VERSTAK
Don't you bet your *fuddler* on zat one, darling.

She ambles off down the narrow passageway between the patients lying on the floor. OGGI stands beside SUSAN. They watch her walk along the center of the hut toward her room at the far end.

EDNA
What's a fuddler?

SUSAN

I think I can guess.

EDNA

Oh, a fuddler.

OGGI

You think she's really a doctor?

SUSAN

What do you mean?

OGGI

Well—who'd know? She's certainly got herself out of working in the fields or cleaning out the lavatory.

INT. BRITISH HUT. NIGHT.

ROSEMARY gestures toward MISS DRUMMOND.

Small homemade gifts are produced and are being handed out to the CHILDREN. MRS. DICKSON, pale and drawn, watches listlessly. ADRIENNE and MRS. PIKE sit beside her. ADRIENNE gives her a small gift.

ADRIENNE

Buck up, Phyllis, it's Christmas.

MRS. DICKSON unwraps the gift as she speaks.

MRS. DICKSON

Where's the champagne? The plum pudding? The turkey? *(She looks at the gift—a small hand-embroidered handkerchief)* . . . Thank you, Adrienne, it's lovely . . . *(She dabs her eyes with it.)*

A few feet away, MRS. ROBERTS is mumbling deliriously, her dog, TILLINGWORTH, nestled beside her. CELIA puts a wet cloth on her MOTHER'S forehead. SUSAN is beside her.

MRS. PIKE

Perhaps now might be a nice time to deal with that dog.

BETT

You know . . . it'd make a nice stew.

CELIA

Oh no.

She looks from person to person, hoping for support. MISS DRUMMOND walks up beside the mat on which MRS. ROBERTS is lying. She speaks quietly.

MISS DRUMMOND

That little dog doesn't eat much.

EDNA

He eats what we could give to the children.

MISS DRUMMOND

But how would Mrs. Roberts cope without him?

SUSAN

She's right, Edna. It'd be the end of her.

EDNA shrugs, the others drift away. MRS. ROBERTS begins to talk incoherently.
She catches sight of WING and MILLIE, across the other side of the hut. They are talking with MRS. CRONJE, who is handing MILLIE a small bedside clock. MRS. ROBERTS beckons CELIA to come closer.

MRS. ROBERTS

This must be the servants' quarters, dear. Tell Chen Li she's only to come when we call . . .

CELIA

Shhsshhh, Mummy. That's not Chen Li. It's Wing.

WING walks over to where MRS. ROBERTS is lying. MILLIE trails after her.

WING

Malaria. Bad. Sorry. Yes.

CELIA nods.

SUSAN

We can't get any quinine. . . .

WING

Ahhhh.

MRS. ROBERTS

I think she's been stealing the sugar again, dear, you have to watch those Chinese . . . Robbie . . .

WING

I get quinine.

EXT. PERIMETER FENCE. NIGHT.

WING sneaks along in a crouch near the darkest part of the perimeter fence. She pauses and looks toward the main gate, where she sees THE SNAKE approach TWO SENTRIES and begin to abuse them. She carefully lifts the first strand of barbed wire and slides underneath. MILLIE holds the wire above her body. WING then carefully lifts and slides underneath the second wire strand.

A YOUNG CHINESE MAN, dressed in black, materializes out of the darkness. Another man is behind him. He and WING have an urgent whispered conversation in a Chinese dialect. It is clear they are bartering. WING hands over some objects, and items are passed from the MEN to her. The alarm clock given to WING by MRS. CRONJE suddenly begins to ring. The CHINESE TRADER tries frantically to switch it off.

There is a yell from the GUARDS at the gate. Shots are fired. Lights sweep along the fence. WING rapidly slides back under the wire, then, staying in the shadows, runs off toward the huts. The CHINESE MEN have taken off in the other direction, toward the forest.

INT. HUT. NIGHT.

WING rushes in, puffing with the effort.

WING

Ohh . . . ohhh . . . not so young no more.

SUSAN looks out toward the fence. It is very dark, but torches are being shone around outside the wire. There is distant chatter in Japanese.

SUSAN

Did they see you?

WING

I tink maybe not . . . they catch them?

SUSAN

Can't tell . . .

WING takes a small bottle from her pocket and hands it to CELIA, who quickly kneels beside her mother and puts the bottle to her lips.

That black market could get us all in trouble. They've warned us.
They'll cut our rations again . . .

Some of the WOMEN mumble agreement with this warning. The light suddenly goes out. Everyone prepares for the night. The hut is dark, with only some light spilling in from the perimeter fence. Voices can still be heard talking in Japanese but are fading away.

MRS. PIKE

Wing . . .

WING looks down at her, not at first understanding her quizzical look.

WING

Ah. Yes . . .

She takes another small bottle from her pocket. It is full of clear liquid. She passes it unostentatiously to MRS. PIKE, who quickly takes a drink. The taste is unfamiliar.

MRS. PIKE

What is it?

WING

Is no more gin. Is sake. Japan drink. Very strong. You no like?

MRS. PIKE

I wouldn't say that.

EXT. COMPOUND. EARLY MORNING.

The Japanese flag is flying. The WOMEN bow. The Japanese, including COLONEL HIROTA; THE SNAKE; BORIS; MR. MOTO; LOFTY; and RAGS watch impassively. Standing slightly apart from the GROUP is an immaculately dressed OFFICER. ADRIENNE looks at him and recognizes him as the man who gave her, SUSAN, and ROSEMARY a lift in his car. This is CAPTAIN TANAKA. ADRIENNE nudges SUSAN and ROSEMARY, who nod, having also recognized TANAKA.

WING

(*whispering*) Kempei-tai.

ADRIENNE

(*whispering*) What's that? Sounds like a Chinese dish.

WING

(*whispering*) Would be better. Is Japan secret police.

COLONEL HIROTA looks toward CAPTAIN TANAKA, who barks an order. Immediately BORIS and MR. MOTO step forward and walk rapidly toward the assembled rows of prisoners. Without hesitation they grab WING, one on either side of her, and march her back out to the space in front of CAPTAIN TANAKA.

TANAKA barks a further order. THE SNAKE picks up a small jerry can by his boot, walks to where a terrified WING is crouching on the ground, and pours the contents all over her. Casually, TANAKA flicks a match onto her. Almost instantly, she is covered in flame.

The WOMEN are horrified by the screams as WING dies in agony.

The JAPANESE watch impassively, though the INTERPRETER, LOFTY, and COLONEL HIROTA find it difficult to maintain their composure. Even THE SNAKE lowers his eyes.

EXT. GRAVESITE. DAY.

There are already a number of graves in a jungle clearing, each of them marked with a simple wooden cross. The new coffin is lowered. MRS. ROBERTS puts her wreath on top. Everyone stands with lowered heads. Although many of the WOMEN are weeping, they are silent. The only sound is a gentle breeze in the palm trees and some tropical birds. The scene is strangely peaceful.

MISS DRUMMOND takes a scrap of paper from a pocket. SISTER WILHELMINA nods.

MISS DRUMMOND

How silent is this place.
The brilliant sunshine filters
through the trees.
The leaves are rustled by a gentle breeze.
A wild and open space,
By shrubs pink-tipped, mauve-
blossomed, is o'ergrown
A hush enfolds me, deep as I have known.
Unbroken save by distant insect's drone.
A jungle clearing.
A track; through which we bear our load
To Him—it is our Paradise Road.
How silent is this place.
How sacred is this place.

ADRIENNE PARGITER looks with renewed interest at the unprepossessing figure of MISS DRUMMOND as, with simplicity but great feeling, she reads the poem.

46

The "showers" are in a small hut with straw matting covering part of the sides. There are three showerheads but a pitifully small water supply, little more than a drip.

MRS. TIPPLER, MRS. PIKE, and BETT are trying to wash themselves under the trickling water when a GROUP OF DUTCH WOMEN enter. One of them, MRS. CRONJE, indicates with sign language it's their turn for the showers. They start to remove their clogs.

MRS. PIKE
One would think they'd have learnt a few words of English by now.

MRS. TIPPLER
They understand a lot more than they let on.

She ungraciously leaves the shower area, followed by the other WOMEN. THE DUTCH move in, talking in their own language.

BETT has picked up her dress, when she turns back and goes to the showers. She pushes her way past the DUTCH WOMEN and looks around.

BETT
Wait a minute. I want my soap. Where's that soap?

MRS. CRONJE
Sop?

She asks the others, in Dutch, what BETT could be talking about. None of them know.

MRS. TIPPLER
Soap. SOAP. What else . . . !

She indicates what it is with a washing action. MRS. CRONJE looks around.

MRS. CRONJE
Ah . . . no. No sop.

BETT
Come on! Don't give me that! It was here . . . right there.

She points to a spot on the floor. MRS. CRONJE looks down, then shrugs.

BETT
I had to write an IOU for five pounds for that soap . . . and I want it NOW!!

MRS. CRONJE can't understand a word and pushes BETT away from her. BETT slips on the wet floor and falls. The other BRITISH WOMEN come forward to help her. As she gets up she pushes MRS. CRONJE.

BETT

You bloody thief!!!

Within seconds a brawl between all the WOMEN has erupted. There is much slapping and abuse in English and Dutch. SISTER WILHELMINA rushes in with a couple of other NUNS, followed by MISS DRUMMOND. They separate the brawling groups, who stand facing one another, panting with indignation. They yell counter-accusations.

SISTER WILHELMINA

Come. . . . Calm. Please. She take your soap. I don't tink so.

MRS. TIPPLER

You don't tink so? I bloody well tink so. Let's look through their ugly bloody dresses or their silly wooden shoes.

As she rants MISS DRUMMOND is looking around the shower area. She leans down into the straw at the side of the shower. She produces the small cake of soap. The protagonists look at one another, still angry, offended. BETT hides her face in embarrassment.

INT. BRITISH HUTS. NIGHT.

Most of the occupants are preparing for bed. MISS DRUMMOND is by her bed, her hands together in prayer. ADRIENNE, who sleeps nearby, is humming a sad melody to herself. She glances at MISS DRUMMOND, who startles her by suddenly speaking.

MISS DRUMMOND

The Elgar concerto.

ADRIENNE

What?

MISS DRUMMOND

You're humming the Elgar concerto.

She continues the theme. ADRIENNE joins her. They hum the haunting theme together.

MISS DRUMMOND

Do you know I went to the first performance—Felix Salmond played it in Leeds. 1920.

49

ADRIENNE smiles. MISS DRUMMOND gets up from her praying position and sits on the end of the bed rostrum.

MISS DRUMMOND
(*continues*) It was almost the last concert for me. The church sent me to China a few months later. . . .

ADRIENNE
But you're not a musician are you, Miss Drummond? Your . . . poem . . . I assumed you taught English.

MISS DRUMMOND
In China I taught a bit of everything, but I studied music at Durham.

ADRIENNE
Miss Drummond, would you care to take a turn with me in the gardens before lights out?

MISS DRUMMOND
I should be delighted, Mrs. Pargiter.

She starts to get up.

ADRIENNE
Oh, I'm so sorry I've interrupted your prayers.

MISS DRUMMOND
Perhaps it's just as well. I was about to ask God to smite Captain Tanaka and The Snake with a severe dysentery.

EXT. CAMP COMPOUND. NIGHT.

Insects hover around the lights of both the perimeter fence and the huts. A few women and children sit by the hut walls, chatting and trying to take advantage of the relative coolness of the evening. JAPANESE GUARDS are by the main gate, smoking, and talking.
MISS DRUMMOND and ADRIENNE walk along by the fence.

ADRIENNE
I studied music at the Royal Academy—under Sir Henry Wood. . . .

MISS DRUMMOND
Do you play the violin? Or viola?

ADRIENNE
Violin? How did you know?

MISS DRUMMOND

Just a guess . . . a few nights ago you were humming Mozart's *Sinfonia Concertante* and . . . It has leads for both instruments.

ADRIENNE

It has leads for both instruments . . . in fact the high point of my career was playing the violin part with Sir Henry conducting.

MISS DRUMMOND hums the main melody for violin and viola from the Mozart *Sinfonia*. ADRIENNE joins her. They both laugh, thoughtfully.

MISS DRUMMOND

Now—you say "high point" of your career? . . .

ADRIENNE

I didn't mean . . . though, you know, I suppose it was. . . . I went to Singapore with my father and met William out there. He's an absolute darling, but . . .

MISS DRUMMOND

Musically, he wouldn't know "God Save the Weasel" from "Pop Goes the King."

ADRIENNE

(*smiles*) No, and music was fairly low on the list of priorities for Singapore society.

MISS DRUMMOND

Very low, judging from the stories I've read by Mr. Somerset Maugham.

ADRIENNE

Oh . . . to read him one would think we did nothing but drink G and T's, murder one another and indulge in ceaseless . . .

She stops herself, aware she is speaking to a missionary.

MISS DRUMMOND

Wife-swapping . . . what will they think of next. . . .

ADRIENNE is put at ease by MISS DRUMMOND'S remark.

ADRIENNE

Do you know, Miss Drummond . . . I feel I owe you an apology.

MISS DRUMMOND

Me!? Whatever for?

ADRIENNE

My . . . snobbery. We never mixed with missionaries in Singapore. We were taught to look down on them.

MISS DRUMMOND

Oh, we're a tedious lot, most of us. And self-righteous.

The lights in their hut flash on and off.
They turn and walk back toward their hut.

MISS DRUMMOND

Do you think the dear old Headmaster would let us have a piano if we asked nicely?

ADRIENNE

No.

MISS DRUMMOND

No. Yes, it would definitely be no . . . Spoilsport.

ADRIENNE begins to hum again.

ADRIENNE

You're not serious.

MISS DRUMMOND

Not really. Well, maybe just a little bit.

The camp lights flicker off and on again. ADRIENNE glances toward the main gate, where THE SNAKE is standing.

ADRIENNE

Oh dear, back we go, or the lead prefect will be after us.

MISS DRUMMOND

Do you know, Mrs. Pargiter, I'vd just had a wonderful idea.

INT/EXT. KITCHEN AREA. MORNING.

ADRIENNE is talking to a GROUP of WOMEN in the large kitchen hut. Most are eating tiny portions of rice with their fingers and drinking rice tea. The group includes ROSEMARY, MRS. O'RIORDEN, MRS. TIPPLER, MRS. PIKE, MRS. DICKSON, and TOPSY MERRITT.

MRS. TIPPLER

An orchestra! You're crazy.

MRS. PIKE

Do you expect the Japanese would give us instruments?

ADRIENNE

Not at all, Harriet. I thought I made it clear.

MISS DRUMMOND

We don't need instruments.

She looks toward MISS DRUMMOND, who is standing at the far side of the GROUP. She nods to ADRIENNE.

TOPSY

Adrienne, I don't think so. After what happened no one's in the mood for a sing-along.

ADRIENNE

But that's the point.

MRS. O'RIORDEN

But I'm thinkin' it's not such a bad idea now.

ADRIENNE

Can you read music, Mrs. O'Riorden?

MRS. O'RIORDEN

Read it? I didn't know you could read it. But I can sing it all right.

ADRIENNE

I think not.

ROSEMARY

I was in the choir at Roedean.

ADRIENNE nods and gives a smile. She looks toward MRS. DICKSON.

ADRIENNE

Phyllis?

MRS. DICKSON

Adrienne—I think it's a . . . harebrained idea. We've hardly got the strength to talk.

MRS. TIPPLER

If you want my advice you'll forget the whole thing. You think the Japs'll agree? Not on your Nellie. . . .

53

MRS. PIKE

(*gently, reminding*) They *have* forbidden any meetings or religious services. We can't even have classes for the children . . .

She looks toward the main gate of the camp, where THE SNAKE is standing, talking to one of the GUARDS.

INT. HUT. NIGHT.

MISS DRUMMOND is writing musical notes on lines she's ruled in a small exercise book. She is arranging the Largo from the *New World Symphony*. She is sitting as close as possible to the one low-wattage bulb hanging in the middle of the hut.

Other WOMEN are sitting around or preparing for bed. It is hot, as usual. A few are eating the remnants of a scanty and ghastly meal.

ADRIENNE looks on as MISS DRUMMOND rapidly fills the staves with music. Nearby SIOBHAN O'RIORDEN is ruling more staves for her on scraps of paper.

ADRIENNE

You must have perfect recall, Miss Drummond. I envy you.

MISS DRUMMOND

They say Mozart could play any piece through after hearing it only once. I'm cheating . . . I know the Dvorak back to front . . . and it's probably full of mistakes.

ADRIENNE

I don't think so. (*She looks over the arrangement of staves on the paper.*) It's quite complicated. I don't envy you conducting it.

MISS DRUMMOND

I should think not. I'm not conducting it, you are.

ADRIENNE looks at her, slightly bewildered.

ADRIENNE

Me!

MISS DRUMMOND

Of course . . . you trained at the Royal Academy.

ADRIENNE

But I was a violinist. And that was years ago.

MISS DRUMMOND

Mrs. Pargiter . . . you read music and Sir Thomas Beecham isn't available.

ADRIENNE looks at her and nods.

ADRIENNE looks around, then walks to the far end of the hut, where SUSAN and EDNA are sitting. She passes ROSEMARY and HELEN. Camera stays with them as ADRIENNE is seen to speak to the two NURSES.

ROSEMARY

After tea we shall go to the Member's Stand and watch the gentlemen play cricket.

HELEN

After tea vee will go to zee . . .

ROSEMARY

We *shall* go to *the* . . . "Shall" is more refined.

HELEN

. . . we shall go to thee Member's Stand and vatch . . .

ROSEMARY

Watch.

HELEN

Watch the gentlemans play ze cricket.

ROSEMARY nods and smiles.

EDNA

What're you gonna sing? I love Rudy Vallee. . . .

ADRIENNE

(*sharply*) It won't be Rudy Vallee.

She turns her attention to MRS. ROBERTS.

ADRIENNE

What about you, Mrs. Roberts?

MRS. ROBERTS

My dear, I was a stalwart of the Cathedral choir in Singapore. My husband, Robbie, head of . . .

CELIA

You have a lovely voice, Mummy.

MRS. ROBERTS

(*grandly*) Perhaps I shall consider it.

ADRIENNE smiles and nods. She crosses the hut to talk to MILLIE and two other ASIAN WOMEN.

MRS. PARGITER

Lovely, I'll put you down.

MRS. ROBERTS

(*cont.*) What kind of people will be in this group? I mean, one doesn't want to mix . . .

CELIA

Mummy!

MRS. ROBERTS

What's wrong? I simply asked what kind of people . . .

CELIA

People like us, Mummy. Prisoners of the Japanese.

MRS. ROBERTS

That's irrelevant, dear. One has a certain . . . position. One can tolerate the Dutch . . . some of them . . . but . . .

She looks again toward the ASIAN WOMEN, who are talking among themselves in Malay, now that ADRIENNE has moved on to other people.

CELIA

Mummy . . .

MRS. ROBERTS

What is it, Celia? Try and finish your sentences.

CELIA

Do you remember Wing?

MRS. ROBERTS

Of course. Horrible business. Horrible. But who knows what contraband she was trading in? Probably some . . . Oriental . . .

CELIA

Quinine, Mummy. She'd gone to get quinine for you.

MRS. ROBERTS

Oh . . .

MRS. TIPPLER walks along the hut to where MISS DRUMMOND is writing the music. She is absorbed and appears not to notice MRS. TIPPLER.

MRS. TIPPLER

You know what Colonel Hirota said about writing anything. They find that they could execute the whole bloody lot of us!

There is a mumble of agreement from a number of people, including MRS. PIKE. SUSAN looks toward ADRIENNE, then toward MISS DRUMMOND.

MRS. PIKE

(*gently*) Perhaps we're all being put in a . . . precarious position, Adrienne.

ADRIENNE

Perhaps. I happen to think it's worth risking.

There is a murmur of discussion. More appear to side with MRS. TIPPLER and MRS. PIKE than ADRIENNE. SUSAN listens for some moments.

SUSAN

The Japanese will only find out if somebody says something.

MRS. TIPPLER

What's that supposed to mean!

MRS. TIPPLER advances on SUSAN and places herself before her. SUSAN looks up into her eyes. She hesitates, then . . .

SUSAN

Somebody tells them every time one of us rolls over in bed. You've always got plenty of cigarettes.

MRS. TIPPLER

Do you think I . . . I've never heard anything so insulting! . . .

SUSAN

Someone told them it was Wing trading through the fence that night.

MRS. TIPPLER

It certainly wasn't me! What about that Jew doctor? What about that one (*she points to Antoinette*) . . . always making eyes at that bloody guard.

ADRIENNE

Susan! Mrs. Tippler! That's enough.

They look at her for a moment. MRS. TIPPLER angrily stomps over to her mat and sits down beside her TWO SONS. SUSAN sits down beside EDNA and OGGI.

EDNA

Strewth! You were the shyest little thing in nursing school. . . .

SUSAN

Maybe nobody there ever got my goat.

EXT. COMPOUND. DAY.

A NUMBER OF WOMEN cross the compound toward the kitchen block.
    THE SNAKE, outside the gate, looks toward them with curiosity.

INT. KITCHEN BLOCK. DAY.

At one end of the large room food is being cleaned and prepared. At the other end all the potential members of the choir have gathered. Many of the familiar faces of the camp are present: DUTCH, BRITISH, AND ASIAN, though not MRS. TIPPLER, MRS. PIKE, or MRS. DICKSON. TOPSY MERRITT is among the GROUP, but with a dubious expression. MRS. ROBERTS, still pale, leans against her daughter, CELIA. ADRIENNE and MISS DRUMMOND face the GROUP; SISTER WILHELMINA stands by to translate into Dutch.
    ADRIENNE sings a brief phrase. Her voice is loud and clear.

ADRIENNE

Who's first? Um. Mrs. O'Riorden, if you would.

MRS. O'RIORDEN copies the phrase.

ADRIENNE

Thank you.

SISTER WILHELMINA

Mrs. Cronje . . .

ADRIENNE

Mrs. Cronje, would you please . . . ?

MRS. O'RIORDEN can't read the music, but is musical and simply repeats the phrase.

The gates open and THE SNAKE directs a GROUP of SIX GUARDS, with bayonets fixed, toward the camp kitchens.

He lets out a fierce samurai scream and heads the charge across the compound. ALL THE GUARDS follow. All screaming.

INT. KITCHEN. DAY.

MRS. CRONJE is singing the phrase. EVERYONE stops and reacts with horror at the screams. Almost immediately, the hut is invaded by THE JAPANESE. They slash their bayonets violently toward the WOMEN. The screaming continues. The meeting breaks up in disarray. SISTER WILHELMINA shoves the music sheets into her habit. THE WOMEN leave the hut from every exit. It is cleared within seconds.

THE SNAKE
No meet!!! You no meet! No like!

INT/EXT. BRITISH HUT. DAY.

MRS. TIPPLER, MRS. PIKE, and a few OTHERS watch the disruption of the choir practice with some amusement.

INT/EXT. HOSPITAL HUT. DAY.

DR. VERSTAK watches the chaos from the hospital hut. SUSAN stops behind her and watches, too.

EXT. COMPOUND. DAY.

EVERYONE leaves the kitchen hut and scatters across the compound or toward their own huts. THE JAPANESE follow, still screaming and thrusting their bayonets at anyone within reach.

THE SNAKE sees MRS. ROBERTS' dog, TILLINGWORTH. He shoots at it. The dog yelps and leaps into the air.

EXT/INT. HOSPITAL HUT. DAY.

On the shaded side of the hut, SUSAN is firmly holding TILLINGWORTH while she stitches up his throat with a needle and thread. He seems to know he's in good hands and lies quietly. OGGI is helping. MRS. ROBERTS watches anxiously.

SUSAN
I reckon he's gonna be all right, Mrs. Roberts. Might have a bit of a funny bark.

She passes the dog back to MRS. ROBERTS, who takes the befuddled creature into her arms and hugs it.

> **MRS. ROBERTS**
> Oh. Thank you, dear.

DR. VERSTAK, who has been watching, comes and sits beside SUSAN. Her face is beaded with sweat.

> **SUSAN**
> Are you okay?

> **DR. VERSTAK**
> Okay. No. Not so okay. But I breaze . . . so is not so bad.

SUSAN is feeling her forehead. She looks into her eyes.

> **SUSAN**
> I think you have a touch of malaria . . . I'll get some. . . .

VERSTAK flinches.

> **DR. VERSTAK**
> I get some whisky. Cures everything . . . After the war, my dear, you go to medical school, yes.

> **SUSAN**
> Me?!

> **DR. VERSTAK**
> You. Why not?

> **SUSAN**
> My father'll want me back on his station. He never even wanted me to go into nursing.

> **DR. VERSTAK**
> Station. He iss a railvay master?

> **SUSAN**
> No. It's a sheep station . . . like a farm.

> **DR. VERSTAK**
> You do vat *you* want, darling. Not vat your father want. He get plenty of those big Australian men to work on ze . . . station.

She looks up to see ADRIENNE, MISS DRUMMOND, and SISTER WILHEL-MINA walking by the perimeter fence.

> **DR. VERSTAK**
> So—der Japanese end der ladies choir before it even begin.

> **ADRIENNE**
> (*correcting her*) Not at all. Vocal orchestra. Not a choir.

MRS. DICKSON, MRS. PIKE, MRS. TIPPLER, and a few OTHERS are in the shower area a short distance away. MRS. DICKSON looks over the top of the cane walls and calls out.

> **MRS. DICKSON**
> But you can't possibly go on with it, Adrienne, not if they won't let everybody meet!

MRS. PIKE and a few of the OTHERS nod in agreement.

> **MISS DRUMMOND**
> It's only the large group that's attracted The Snake's attention.

> **MRS. TIPPLER**
> If you don't care about the rest of us. About the whole camp.

> **ADRIENNE**
> I beg your pardon.

> **MRS. TIPPLER**
> Isn't all this just so you can lord it over the rest of us? Boss everyone around?

> **MRS. DICKSON**
> The whole thing might be a bit grandiose, Adrienne. How many *women* conductors are there anyway?

ADRIENNE looks toward MISS DRUMMOND. She shakes her head.

> **ADRIENNE**
> None that I know of.

> **MISS DRUMMOND**
> This is probably a first. Something to be proud of.

EXT. SHADE OF TREE. DAY.

A group of nine WOMEN, plus ADRIENNE, are under a tree rehearsing for the choir, but are also sewing (with various improvised needles on an odd assortment of pieces of cloth) in order to appear to the GUARDS as a discussion group. The GROUP includes SISTER WILHELMINA, TOPSY, MILLIE, and two other NUNS, MRS. CRONJE, MRS. ROBERTS, and CELIA.

ADRIENNE and the GROUP are doing vocal warm-ups. Their voices run up and down the scales. ADRIENNE looks keenly from one to the other, assessing their abilities.

MRS. ROBERTS looks down at the intricate embroidery MILLIE is doing. MILLIE catches her eye and smiles.

                    ADRIENNE
    Same section. Once more.

They sing a brief phrase.

                    ADRIENNE
    Mrs. Roberts, you're coming in late . . .

                    MRS. ROBERTS
    Oh, I don't think so, dear.

                    ADRIENNE
    Yes, Mrs. Roberts. You must watch me.

                    MRS. ROBERTS
    Oh, I am, dear. Perhaps everyone else was early?

                    ADRIENNE
    No, Mrs. Roberts . . . again . . .

She begins to conduct the phrase. She looks toward MRS. ROBERTS, who is late again.

                    INT. KITCHEN. DAY.

SIOBHAN glances across the compound and sees THE SNAKE striding toward them.

                    SIOBHAN
    Sssssss. The Snake.

Instantly the GROUP of eight singers meld in with THE KITCHEN STAFF. THE SNAKE enters. He stops by the door and looks around, seeing only a GROUP of WOMEN cooking food, peeling, cleaning, washing plates. He stares for a moment, appears to be about to say something, but turns abruptly and strides back angrily across the compound toward the gate.

EXT. OFFICER'S HOUSE. NIGHT.

There is a heavy tropical downpour. THE SNAKE and CAPTAIN TANAKA come onto the verandah. TANAKA is smoking a cigarette. They look toward the camp.

EXT. CAMP. DAY.

It is no longer raining, but the ground is muddy. THE SNAKE waits impatiently for the main gate to be unlocked. He yells angrily at the soldier fumbling with the lock.

He quickly crosses the compound. Children pause in a game to watch him. He pushes a COUPLE of WOMEN out of the way.

INT/EXT. BRITISH HUT. DAY.

THE SNAKE reaches the end of the hut where a GROUP of ladies (including MRS. DICKSON, MRS. PIKE, and MRS. ROBERTS) are playing cards. He screams for attention, whacking his cane down hard on one of the beds. MISS DRUMMOND quickly conceals the music paper on which she was working, and stands up as he approaches. She bows.

MISS DRUMMOND
Is there something we can do for you, Sergeant Tomayashi?

THE SNAKE stares at her for a moment, her quiet manner the perfect antidote to his temper. He pauses, then reaches into his pocket and pulls out a piece of paper. He thrusts it into her hand and marches off.

EXT/INT. HUT. DUSK.

EVERYONE has returned from work duties. A large GROUP is examining the paper, which is a list of names written on an official-looking piece of paper. Japanese characters are across the top, plus the words "Palembang Internment Camp No. 32" and a date, 16th August, 1943. The WOMEN speak quickly, interrupting one another.

ADRIENNE
It's not just choir members, is it? . . . (*she looks at the names*) No . . . I can't see what it means. Do they have something in common?

A murmur as they examine the list. No one seems to think so.

MRS. DICKSON
Some of the Dutch girls are on here, too.

SUSAN
Repatriations?

BETT
Executions?

CELIA
You're there, Rosemary.

ROSEMARY
And so is Susan. And Topsy.

TOPSY is still lying down.

TOPSY
I know . . . God, what else can they do to us?

SUSAN
(*reading*) . . . the main gate at 8:30 . . . after Tenko . . .

MRS. O'RIORDEN
Better not to go. Just don't go.

MRS. DICKSON
No . . . I mean, just say you have another engagement.

ADRIENNE
A mistake, I think.

SISTER WILHELMINA
Oh, they will do something awful to us if we don't go.

MISS DRUMMOND is at the edge of the GROUP.

MISS DRUMMOND
I know what this is.

They quieten and look at her. SUSAN looks at the list again.

SUSAN
What?

MISS DRUMMOND

This is all of the younger girls . . . the more attractive ones.

There is a pause. They realize this is correct.

MRS. TIPPLER

(*calling*) Am I on there?

EVERYONE

No!!

EXT. ROAD. DAY.

A truck speeds along over the potholed road, past an occasional thatched house. A few local inhabitants watch, only mildly interested.

INT. TRUCK. DAY.

The WOMEN, crowded in the back, bounce around. TWO JAPANESE GUARDS sit mutely at the rear. Nobody speaks.

EXT. LARGE HOUSE. DAY.

The truck pulls up outside a large Dutch Colonial house.

INT. LARGE HOUSE. DAY.

THE WOMEN enter a large living room. It is attractively furnished in Dutch style with Oriental additions of paper lanterns and screens. The lighting is dim and atmospheric. COLONEL HIROTA points to a table laden with food. He speaks.

INTERPRETER

This is Japanese Officers Club.

A GROUP of FIVE JAPANESE MEN emerge from another room and stand in an archway. They bow. They are dressed in freshly pressed uniforms. Their boots shine. Their hair is slick and oiled.

INTERPRETER

This is Japanese officer men. Most well-educated and refined. Some speak English like Englishmen from Oxford. Japanese officer look for volunteer to work in club. Volunteer have plenty food and satin sheet.

ADRIENNE

And we are the . . . acceptable "volunteers."

THE INTERPRETER looks toward COLONEL HIROTA.

INTERPRETER

That is . . . correct interpretation.

The WOMEN cluster in a GROUP to discuss the matter, which is also translated into Dutch and the various Asian languages as it is explained to the non-English speakers.

MRS. O'RIORDEN

Disgustin', I call it.

EDNA

I'd rather kiss a leper from Leopoldville before I let any of that lot touch me.

CELIA

Well, we don't *have* to stay. They're not forcing us.

TOPSY

Food. Satin sheets.

THE SNAKE barks out something in Japanese.

INTERPRETER

Ladies who stay in beautiful house all please to walk in direction indicated.

THE SNAKE points to the far side of the room.

There is more discussion, but, slowly, a GROUP of about TWENTY WOMEN—British, Asian, and Dutch—detach themselves from the GROUP and walk across the room. Among them is BETT, trying to lose herself among the GROUP. SUSAN rushes to her.

SUSAN

Bett! You can't be serious?!

BETT

Too right. I am. You know bloody well we've got Buckley's chance of getting through the war in that camp. You think I want to end up in some shallow grave in Sumatra! No fear.

MRS. O'RIORDEN

But the war's going to be finished soon. . . .

You said that over a year ago.

The GUARDS quickly move to push those who choose not to stay back out-side toward the truck.

TOPSY
(*calling*) Hot water. Is there hot water in this club?

INTERPRETER
Plenty hot water. Plenty soap.

After a moment's hesitation, TOPSY steps forward. ADRIENNE puts her arm out and blocks her.

ADRIENNE
Topsy. You can't!

TOPSY
Why not? . . . Are Japanese officers going to be any worse than most of the creeps we've all known?

ADRIENNE
Probably. And what about Marty?

TOPSY
Well (*shrugs*), what he don't know . . .

She turns to go. THE SNAKE and BORIS are impatient and snap at AD-RIENNE in Japanese, clearly telling her she is to leave. She looks at TOPSY, then at the others.

ADRIENNE
Well, what about our vocal orchestra? We'll be an alto short if you go.

TOPSY looks at her incredulously.

TOPSY
You're asking me to give up food and soap and God knows what else so I can starve and sing!?

ADRIENNE
Yes. I suppose I am.

INTERPRETER

Lady, please.

TOPSY looks toward the truck, then back toward ADRIENNE.
She buries her face in ADRIENNE'S shoulder, weeping.

EXT. GARDEN DAY.

SISTER WILHELMINA, SISTER ANNA, and TWO of the other NUNS are
tending the vegetable garden. A group of the women who have been to the
Officers Club are gathered around.

MRS. O'RIORDEN

A good Catholic sister like you! I just can't believe you're not
more . . . more . . .

ADRIENNE

Censorious.

ADRIENNE is merely supplying the word. There is no suggestion she shares
the moral condemnation. MRS. O'RIORDEN is unsure of the exact meaning
of the word, but nods, assuming it is what she means.

SISTER WILHELMINA

I am not zere Judge. Zey want to survive. Zis way . . . maybe zey
will.

MISS DRUMMOND

The will to survive is very strong. Stronger than anything.

MRS. O'RIORDEN

I just can't believe what yer sayin'.

ADRIENNE turns to MRS. DICKSON.

ADRIENNE

Very well, Phyllis, I've lost four sopranos in that lot. You'll have to
join us now.

MRS. DICKSON

Me! I'm not interested in your bloody choir!

ADRIENNE

Well, you can stop lying around and whingeing and get interested.
(*she turns to Susan*) What about you?

OGGI

Not me.

SUSAN

To be honest, I don't like that kind of music you're doing. It's got no tune.

ADRIENNE

You don't know what you're talking about.

SUSAN

No?

ADRIENNE

No.

INT. BRITISH HUT. NIGHT.

ADRIENNE is rehearsing a group of eight that includes MRS. DICKSON, SUSAN, TOPSY, and MISS DRUMMOND. MRS. DICKSON and SUSAN are full of enthusiasm.

A brief phrase is sung.

EXT. HOSPITAL BUILDING—MORTUARY. DAY.

SUSAN crosses from one building to the other. Outside the mortuary a group of CHILDREN are making coffins from bits of old tin and packing cases, bamboo, palm fronds, etc. Among those working are DANNY and MICHAEL TIPPLER, SIOBHAN and ARAN O'RIORDEN.

SIOBHAN

How many you have today?

MICHAEL

Two. I found them first. They were just staring up. Like this.

He imitates the glassy stare of death.

DANNY

Just wait until Mrs. van der Weyden dies. She's so big with beri beri it'll take ten people just to carry her out of the hut!

SUSAN passes the group and goes into the building.

MICHAEL

We'll have to jump on her to squeeze her into the coffin.

70

INT. HOSPITAL MORTUARY. DAY.

The room is kept very dark so that it is as cool as possible to prevent deterioration of the bodies prior to burial.

SUSAN enters and looks around the gloom. Half a dozen bodies are lying on tables. They are not covered. Their emaciated faces stare upward at the corrugated tin roof. She shudders. Coming inside from the bright sun means it takes some seconds for her eyes to adjust to the gloom.

                    SUSAN
Dr. Verstak . . .

                    DR. VERSTAK
Yes. How it goes? The English ladies choir?

                    SUSAN
I can't tell. Seems to be a lot of stopping and starting and no singing.
You sound very disapproving.

                    DR. VERSTAK
But I am not. It keeps de ladies busy and dat is good . . . but de noise
dey will make . . . not for someone who heard de great choirs of
Leipzig . . . Vienna . . .

SUSAN looks down at what DR. VERSTAK is doing to one of the bodies. She
has a hammer and screwdriver in her hands.

                    SUSAN
Why are you . . . ? You're pulling out their gold fillings!

                    DR. VERSTAK
Quite right, my dear. They are of no further use . . . to their owners.

She aims with the hammer at the screwdriver and gives it a bang, then
reaches into the mouth and grabs a tooth.

                    DR. VERSTAK
You should not be so squeamish. With all that you have seen.

                    SUSAN
I think this takes the cake. So this is how you get your whisky and
cigarettes!

                    DR. VERSTAK
That is so. And the small amount of medicine we have. How you
think we get that? The Japanese give it to us? I trade with the guards.

71

SUSAN shakes her head. DR. VERSTAK gives a sharp pull on the tooth. It is still tight. She reaches for a pair of hand-made pliers.

> **DR. VERSTAK**
> Amazing how strong . . . Anyvay, best you know all zis . . . if anything happen to me.

> **SUSAN**
> What do you mean? I should carry on . . . doing this?!

With apprehension, she looks around the dark room, the emaciated bodies staring upward.

> **DR. VERSTAK**
> Only if you want some of de ladies in de camp to stay alive.

She pulls again on the gold tooth. It comes out.

> **DR. VERSTAK**
> So. Vat do you sing?

> **SUSAN**
> Oh. . . . It's all stuff I've never heard. (*She thinks.*) Umm. The *New World*. Dvor . . . (*She can't recall the name.*)

> **DR. VERSTAK**
> Dvorak. Dey sing Dvorak. You don't know Dvorak? It . . . Dey don't teach you anysing in Australia? Only about sheep?

VERSTAK hands SUSAN the teeth.

EXT. CAMP. NIGHT.

Under a starry sky the camp is asleep. All lights are out, except for those around the perimeter fence.

EXT. TOILET BLOCK. NIGHT.

As ADRIENNE exits from the toilets, BORIS grabs her from behind, puts one hand over her mouth, and tries to drag her back inside the building. She struggles fiercely, managing to bite his hand so hard he lets go. She then spins around and slaps him across the face. Already unsteady, he loses his balance and staggers backward, ending up in the latrine. ADRIENNE watches as, screaming garbled abuse in Japanese, he surfaces through the effluent.

Attracted by the noise, some WOMEN—including SISTER WILHEL-MINA, SUSAN, and ROSEMARY—come from the other huts. TWO of the

GUARDS (MR. MOTO and RAGS) come from the main gate to the toilet block.

EXT. BACK OF JAPANESE OFFICER'S HOUSE. DAY.

CAPTAIN TANAKA waits as THE SNAKE unlocks a bamboo cage in which ADRIENNE is imprisoned. The cage is sitting in the sun, out of sight of the camp compound. ADRIENNE has been some hours in the cage. Her skin is burnt and she is dehydrated and disoriented. Her hair has been roughly chopped short by her captors.

Standing behind TANAKA is a rather chastened-looking BORIS.

> **TANAKA**
> I have perhaps seen you before?

> **ADRIENNE**
> I think not.

> **TANAKA**
> I think so. The insolent lady to whom I gave a ride.

ADRIENNE returns his stare, but says nothing.

> **TANAKA**
> Japanese soldier *never* attack women. You refused to bow to him. He struck you on the face. Quite rightly. Then you struck him.

> **ADRIENNE**
> No. He was drunk. I could smell the sake. He grabbed me from be-hind and . . .

Before she can finish TANAKA hits her brutally across the face. She falls back against the cage and then to the ground. . . . He walks over to her and kicks her in the ribs. She groans in pain.

INT. COLONEL HIROTA'S OFFICE. DAY.

COLONEL HIROTA is feeding worms to some caged birds by the window of his office. He looks around as he hears footsteps on the verandah of his house. The INTERPRETER looks apologetically into the room. Behind him are SISTER WILHELMINA, SUSAN, and MISS DRUMMOND. THE SNAKE, who has escorted them to the house, remains outside the door as COLONEL HIROTA curtly indicates they are to enter the room and sit. He sits across the desk from them. A fan blows a cool breeze onto him across a block of ice.

COLONEL HIROTA speaks in Japanese.

INTERPRETER
Colonel Hirota says incident with lady most regrettable, but is death for strike Japanese soldier. Lady have very bad manners. Manners very important to Japanese people.

COLONEL HIROTA says something curtly in Japanese. His manner indicates, with a gesture, that the interview is at an end. He looks down toward his desk. SUSAN stands and looks down at him.

SUSAN
You are starving and beating women and children! You don't give us any medicine for the sick. Not even quinine for the bloody malaria everyone's got. You steal our Red Cross parcels for yourselves. You make us work like slaves. You won't let us write to our families and . . . and you have the cheek to lecture us on good manners!

There is a silence. THE SNAKE, who watched SUSAN'S outburst with awe, looks from her to the INTERPRETER to COLONEL HIROTA. The INTER-PRETER does not translate into Japanese, but looks helplessly at COLONEL HIROTA, who cannot fail to have understood the essence of SUSAN'S tirade. He speaks briefly in Japanese. The INTERPRETER hesitates, then lowers his eyes as he translates.

INTERPRETER
Tomorrow lady will be executed.

SISTER WILHELMINA

Please. You tell Colonel Hirota that I saw vat happen. The colonel knows that I am a nun and nuns never tell lie . . . the lady only raises her hands to protect herself. Like this. (*She demonstrates by raising her hands across her face.*) And when she hit him is by accident. He fall back into the latrine. (*Her gesture indicates the fall into the latrine.*)

THE INTERPRETER nervously translates this to COLONEL HIROTA. SISTER WILHELMINA watches, her face radiating candor.

INTERPRETER

Colonel Hirota say he regrets. But matter all dealt with by Captain Tanaka. Captain Tanaka with Kempei-tai . . .

THE INTERPRETER'S tone indicates this is the end of the discussion. Even his pronunciation of "kempei-tai" is awestruck.

MISS DRUMMOND has stood quietly throughout.

COLONEL HIROTA is turning away from the women as she speaks, quietly.

MISS DRUMMOND

Oh, so Captain Tanaka is in charge of this camp? I understood it was you, Colonel Hirota. . . .

COLONEL HIROTA insists on a translation. THE INTERPRETER reluctantly complies.

INT. HOSPITAL. LATE AFTERNOON.

SUSAN is binding some cloth around ADRIENNE. SISTER WILHELMINA, DR. VERSTAK, and MISS DRUMMOND are watching. DR. VERSTAK is smoking, though she is cold and shaking with malaria. A ragged blanket is around her shoulders.

DR. VERSTAK

Two broken ribs is not so bad. Better than . . . (*She lifts her hand and makes a severing motion.*) Yes? You will not be able to move around for maybe a week. Maybe two.

ADRIENNE

That's impossible. Everything is arranged for Saturday. It's our anniversary.

DR. VERSTAK

Anniversary?

MISS DRUMMOND
We'll have been here for two years.

DR. VERSTAK
Vot an anniversary! You do as you like. I am only the doctor.

SISTER WILHELMINA
I tell a lie. But God vill forgive me. I think perhaps he even congratulate me.

DR. VERSTAK
I have some medicine. Come.

They follow her to the partitioned off section at the end of the room. SUSAN helps ADRIENNE. DR. VERSTAK takes a bottle of whisky out from under the bedclothes. She pours a dash into each of four containers. Offers one to SISTER WILHELMINA.

DR. VERSTAK
Sister?

MRS. PARGITER
Cheers. (*She takes a big swig.*)

SISTER WILHELMINA
Whisky—I love whisky. I am a nun, not a saint.

DR. VERSTAK turns to MISS DRUMMOND.

DR. VERSTAK
And you, are you a saint?

MISS DRUMMOND
No, that will make me fall over.

DR. VERSTAK pours her a dash of whisky.

SUSAN
I've never drunk whisky.

DR. VERSTAK
And let us hope zat you do vorse things in your life. (*She lifts her glass.*) Prost.

SISTER WILHELMINA
Proost.

ADRIENNE

Cheers.

SUSAN

Bottoms up.

MISS DRUMMOND

Faith. (*She drinks.*) You can do very little with it . . . but nothing without it.

They all drink.

DR. VERSTAK

Japanese visky. Not Scotch. Still—vee can't have everysing.

INT. BRITISH HUT. NIGHT.

Almost everyone is dressing up as much as possible. Clothes have been cleaned and stitched. Special dresses and uniforms brought from their hiding places. WOMEN are combing and brushing one another's hair, checking each other's makeup.

MILLIE and MRS. ROBERTS are still side by side on a mat. MRS. ROBERTS is embroidering. MILLIE watches attentively. . . . She nods approvingly.

CELIA, dressed up for the evening, passes by.

The THREE AUSTRALIAN NURSES have one brilliant orange lipstick which they apply to one another's lips.

OGGI

You got some lipstick.

SUSAN

Orange. All the rage in Palembang.

EDNA

It's been a long time since I kissed a man. There's nothing nicer.

They all giggle.

INT. DUTCH HUT. NIGHT.

ALL OF THE NUNS are ready, their habits sparkling. ROSEMARY is combing HELEN'S hair.

ROSEMARY

You look lovely, Helen. Some man will be very lucky one day.

HELEN

Not if we stay here. We meet no vun.

ROSEMARY

(*correcting*) We shall not meet anyone. (*She articulates the word very clearly.*) But we won't stay in here. One day we'll all go home.

EXT. COMPOUND. NIGHT.

WOMEN exit all of the huts and head toward the large central kitchen. At the gates two of the GUARDS watch, puzzled. THE SNAKE joins them. He looks curiously toward the procession of oddly well-dressed ladies. GUARDS look to him for orders but he continues to stare at the WOMEN.

INT. KITCHEN. NIGHT.

ALMOST THE ENTIRE CAMP has gathered. There are a few stools and chairs but most people are sitting on the floor.

At the end of the room the thirty-strong choir is gathering, facing the audience. There is a low murmur of anticipation.

INT. HUT. NIGHT.

MRS. TIPPLER, MRS. PIKE, and one or two others sit by themselves.

MRS. TIPPLER

There's going to be trouble. Japs won't take this lying down.

The other WOMEN nod their agreement.

MRS. TIPPLER'S two sons, who have been standing at the end of the room, suddenly exchange a nod and dash off in the direction everyone else has been going. MRS. TIPPLER looks at MRS. PIKE and the other WOMEN and shrugs.

EXT. GATE. NIGHT.

Six GUARDS are now gathered and are looking toward the kitchen area in the middle of the compound. THE SNAKE gives an order and the gate is unlocked.

INT. KITCHEN. NIGHT.

ADRIENNE walks to the center of the floor, she turns and faces the GROUP. She is still in some pain, but manages to conceal it. A baton is in her hand. The room quietens.

EXT. COMPOUND. NIGHT.

THE SNAKE gives an order. The JAPANESE GUARDS quickly cross the compound.

THE SNAKE remains, watching, by the main gate.

INT. KITCHEN. NIGHT.

The ASSEMBLED CHOIR hold their music sheets in front of them. All their eyes are on Adrienne.

The JAPANESE SOLDIERS burst into the kitchen area and look, in amazement, at the large assembly. Just as the corporal in charge (MR. MOTO) is about to scream a command, ADRIENNE drops her baton and the choir begins a wordless (and instrumentless) version of the Largo from Dvorak's *New World Symphony*. (NB. *The various choir rehearsals, prior to this scene, have all been staged in such a way that the music has been presented only in fragments, in order that the impact of the full choir will not be diminished*). THE CORPORAL slowly closes his mouth. He looks around at the other SOLDIERS, all of whom are standing transfixed, captivated, as is the audience, by the growing beauty of Dvorak's glorious melodies.

The choir includes MISS DRUMMOND, ANTOINETTE, HELEN, SUSAN, MRS. DICKSON, EDNA, MICHELE, TOPSY, MILLIE, SISTER WILHELMINA, SISTER ANNA, THREE OTHER NUNS, MRS. CRONJE, ROSEMARY, MRS. ROBERTS (clutching her dog), CELIA ROBERTS, MRS. O'RIORDEN, and her daughter SIOBHAN, BEATRICE, and MAVIS.

The camp and the horrors of camp life are forgotten as everyone listens to the choir. Tears stream down the faces of many of the listeners. THE JAPANESE GUARDS slowly put down their rifles, then squat on the floor and listen to the music. LOFTY can't take his eyes from ANTOINETTE.

INT. BRITISH HUT. NIGHT.

MRS. TIPPLER and the WOMEN can hear the music. They are unimpressed.

EXT. GATE. NIGHT.

THE SNAKE is still at the gate to the camp. He listens, too, but impassively.

INT. HOSPITAL. NIGHT.

WOMEN lying in the beds can hear the music. DR. VERSTAK, ill in bed in her small partitioned room at the end of the building, props herself up on her elbow and looks across to the kitchen. She is smoking, as usual. She is stunned by the quality of the singing—the technical perfection, the emotional force.

EXT. JAPANESE OFFICERS' HOUSE. NIGHT.

CAPTAIN TANAKA is on the verandah, looking toward the camp. He can hear the choir. COLONEL HIROTA, from the doorway, speaks to him in Japanese.

EXT. CAMP. NIGHT.

Wide shot of the camp and the countryside beyond. The music continues.

EXT. GRAVEYARD, NIGHT.

The graveyard is now full of crosses made of twigs. Music continues.

INT. KITCHEN. NIGHT.

The Dvorak continues and then finishes. For a moment there is silence, and then rapturous applause. In sheer joy, the WOMEN all rush to embrace one another.

EXT. ROAD OUTSIDE CAMP. DAY.

MRS. O'RIORDEN
(*She drinks, then passes the bottle back to Antoinette.*) I'm fallin' down like an old house. . . . Look at my legs! (*She pushes her tattered skirt to*

one side and shows her bony legs and knobby knees.) I look like that little wooden man.

ROSEMARY

Pinocchio.

MRS. O'RIORDEN

That's the fellah.

HELEN looks back in the direction of the camp and nods to the others. They look, to see THE SNAKE approaching.

TOPSY

Uh-oh. The winner of the 1944 Dale Carnegie Charm School Award. Tokyo Division.

THE SNAKE screams orders, in his usual style. The TWO JAPANESE GUARDS sitting down rapidly get to their feet and indicate to the WOMEN they are to leave.

As they start to walk off back to the camp, THE SNAKE screams again.

THE SNAKE

You!!

The WOMEN look around. He points to ADRIENNE.

THE SNAKE

You!!! You no go!!

Everyone hesitates with apprehension. THE SNAKE yells again, in Japanese, and the GUARDS push the others off down the road. ADRIENNE indicates they must leave. She turns and faces THE SNAKE. He gestures to the GUARDS who came in with him to leave also. They, too, walk off back to the camp.

THE SNAKE and ADRIENNE are left alone on the road. The other WOMEN turn back to look at them. They exchange glances.

THE SNAKE takes his rifle from his shoulder and indicates to ADRIENNE she is to take a narrow path into the forest.

EXT. FOREST. DAY.

Tense, but calm, ADRIENNE walks along in front of THE SNAKE. She looks from side to side, wondering if she could dive into the jungle and make her escape. She decides it's impossible. He would be able to shoot her within seconds.

Some distance from the road he tells her to stop. He points to a tree, indicating she is to sit by it. Apprehensively, she does so.

81

He advances toward her, then squats down a few feet away, facing her. For a few moments they stare at one another. Then, to her amazement, he begins to sing. It is a Japanese folk song, sentimental and melodic.

He finishes the song and stares at her. His eyes are full of tears.

THE SNAKE
You like?

ADRIENNE nods.

EXT. PATH TO CAMP. DAY.

The other WOMEN are walking back along the roadway. As they round a bend TWO CHINESE MEN are standing by the side of the road. They both bow to the JAPANESE GUARDS. One of them hands a piece of paper surreptitiously to MILLIE. She takes it deftly, then peeks at it. She catches up with ROSEMARY and slips it into her hand.

The choir singing Chopin's *Funeral March Prelude* is heard.

INT. BRITISH HUT. DAY.

ROSEMARY is sitting on her mat. MILLIE approaches and pushes the note into her hand.

MILLIE
Is for you.

ROSEMARY looks at her quizzically.

MILLIE
From Chinese man . . .

ROSEMARY unfolds the piece of paper and reads it.

DENNIS *(Voiceover)*
My darling. I hope this finds you well. I'm in camp at Telamatu. I'm escaping with some of the Aussies. See you in Sydney. Hotel Australia. All my love.

INT. KITCHEN. NIGHT.

The choir is singing Chopin's *Funeral March Prelude.*

INT. KITCHEN AREA. NIGHT.

The choir is singing *Bolero.* Almost the whole camp is attending and listens with rapture and pride. The piece is flawless. Even SUSAN and MRS. ROB-

ERTS manage their entrances at exactly the right time. ADRIENNE permits herself a smile of relief. MISS DRUMMOND sings as lustily as ever but is sitting down to do so. DR. VERSTAK, pale and thin, with an army blanket around her shoulders listens with pleasure.

This time COLONEL HIROTA and THE INTERPRETER are sitting in the front row. COLONEL HIROTA is immaculately dressed, his hair slicked down, his boots polished.

EXT. CAMP GATES. NIGHT.

THE SNAKE stands by the gate listening to the music. He is smoking a cigarette, his face expressionless. A soldier walks up and asks him something. His only reply is to box the man's ears, quickly and viciously.

INT. CAMP KITCHEN. NIGHT.

The music ends in a massive crescendo. At first there is a stunned silence. A roar of applause follows. The JAPANESE applaud politely, taking their cue from COLONEL HIROTA, who speaks to THE INTERPRETER.

INT. HUT. NIGHT.

There are only a few occupants. Most of them too ill to attend the concert.

MRS. TIPPLER
It's just humming, that's all. Anybody could do that.

INT. CAMP KITCHEN. NIGHT.

The applause continues. It is especially directed at ADRIENNE and MISS DRUMMOND. They bow.

ADRIENNE
Do you know, Miss Drummond, I don't know your Christian name.

MISS DRUMMOND
It's Daisy, but I've always hated it. I want to be called Margaret.

ADRIENNE
Then it's Margaret. Why not?

THE INTERPRETER walks up to them. He presents ADRIENNE with two small cakes of soap.

INTERPRETER
A gift from Colonel Hirota.

83

ADRIENNE

Tell him "thank you." This will go a long way among three hundred of us.

INTERPRETER

Colonel Hirota says you will please to sing one Japanese folk song.

ADRIENNE

Tell him "no."

INTERPRETER

Oh . . . but . . . this is very difficult . . .

ADRIENNE

Tell him my appreciation of Japanese culture is at a low ebb.

INTERPRETER

I think I make some . . . other reason . . .

ADRIENNE

As you wish.

The INTERPRETER leaves, nervously heading for COLONEL HIROTA. AD-RIENNE turns and catches MISS DRUMMOND'S glance.

ADRIENNE

You don't hate them, do you? Why not?

MISS DRUMMOND

I can't bring myself to hate people. I've tried, but the worse they behave, the sorrier I feel for them.

EXT. COMPOUND. EARLY MORNING.

The WOMEN are bowing to the Japanese flag.

ROSEMARY

(under her breath) Bugger the Emperor.

ADRIENNE

(under her breath) Bugger the Emperor.

SUSAN

(whispering) Fancy having a flag with a poached egg on it.

CAPTAIN TANAKA glances toward her, although it's unlikely he could have heard her comment.

As always, COLONEL HIROTA is facing the assembled WOMEN. THE INTERPRETER is to one side of him. CAPTAIN TANAKA stands, immaculately attired, on the other side.

INTERPRETER

Colonel Hirota proud to report further victory of Japanese Armed Forces. . . . American Imperialists removed from many Pacific island and bomb Australia many time. Australia government want to make peace with Japan.

SUSAN

(not too softly) That will be the day.

CAPTAIN TANAKA glances toward SUSAN.

INTERPRETER

Churchill and Roosevelt number ten. Emperor Hirohito, the Son of Heaven, number one.

Everyone is silent. COLONEL HIROTA turns and walks back toward the gates of the compound. He is followed by THE INTERPRETER and some of the GUARDS. THE SNAKE dismisses the WOMEN. As the lines break up a voice screams out.

TANAKA

You! You stay!!!

Everyone freezes. CAPTAIN TANAKA points toward SUSAN MACARTHY.
    Everyone watches, uncertain what is going to happen. TANAKA stares at SUSAN for some moments. She returns his gaze.

TANAKA

You spoke. What did you say?

SUSAN

I said, warm, isn't it? For this time of year!

TANAKA stares at her a moment longer. Then he barks an order to THE SNAKE.

EXT. CAMP. DAY.

SUSAN is kneeling in the sun. Pieces of razor-sharp wood have been placed behind her legs, so that if she moves backward her skin will be sliced. WOMEN watch from the huts. They are kept at a distance by a GUARD.

EXT/INT. HOSPITAL. DAY.

DR. VERSTAK looks toward SUSAN from the hospital. She shrugs and turns away from the sight.

EXT. CAMP COMPOUND. LATER STILL. SAME DAY

SUSAN is becoming severely burnt. She forces herself to stay upright. MISS DRUMMOND walks toward her with a tin helmet full of water. THE SNAKE is standing by the main gate. He looks toward the officers' house, sees CAP-TAIN TANAKA, then yells out loudly to the guard, LOFTY.

Reluctantly, LOFTY walks to MISS DRUMMOND and takes the water from her.

LOFTY

(quietly) Sorry. Sorry.

EXT. CAMP COMPOUND. NIGHT.

ADRIENNE, ROSEMARY, and some of the OTHERS look from the hut to see SUSAN still kneeling in the same position in the middle of the night. A guard, RAGS, is standing a few yards from her.

INT. HOSPITAL. NIGHT.

DR. VERSTAK is in her room at the end of the hospital. She is standing, facing the INTERPRETER.

DR. VERSTAK

You say to Captain Tanaka that all wars end. You tell him that per-haps the invincible Japanese army will lose this one. Who knows? And if they do then his treatment of this young woman *(she points to the compound where SUSAN is kneeling)* will not result in the Allies building any shrines to him. Maybe they even hang him. Yes.

The INTERPRETER is not delighted at being asked to convey this message. He sweats with anxiety.

INTERPRETER

I do not think . . . you are in a position to . . . threaten Captain Ta-naka.

DR. VERSTAK

Oh, not a threat. Advice only. I am his ally. You tell him.

INTERPRETER

I think is impossible . . .

DR. VERSTAK
I can understand this. But . . . you try. Yes?

The INTERPRETER nervously looks toward her and then toward the compound.

EXT. CAMP. LATE AFTERNOON.

SUSAN is still kneeling, but is staying upright only with tremendous effort. She is semiconscious. Most of the camp watch her silently. They look toward the gate as it opens and CAPTAIN TANAKA enters, followed by TWO GUARDS. TANAKA strides up toward SUSAN and stands to one side of her. He looks at her for some moments, pleased at her pitiful condition.

There is a gasp as TANAKA unsheathes the samurai sword by his side.

He raises the sword above his head. A gasp runs through the watching crowd. SUSAN turns her head, painfully, looks him in the eye, but says nothing. TANAKA looks down at the kneeling figure. His eye takes in her neck. The camp goes completely silent, the only sound being the wind as it blows dust around the onlookers. No one moves.

Suddenly, TANAKA swings the sword down. A lock of hair falls from SUSAN'S head to the ground. There is a gasp from the crowd, then a further moment of silence before they realize that SUSAN is unharmed.

TANAKA turns abruptly and strides away, back out through the main gate. ADRIENNE and ROSEMARY rush to help SUSAN to her feet—a slow process as her limbs are stiff and cramped.

ADRIENNE
Well, that's one to tell your grandchildren.

SUSAN
(weakly) I knew he was bluffing. . . .

EXT. CAMP. PRE-DAWN.

All is quiet. The main gate is opened and the GUARDS come through yelling loudly to wake everyone. When they reach the huts they kick their feet against the walls.

EXT. COMPOUND. DAWN.

The WOMEN are being herded into trucks with innumerable yells, pushes, and slaps from the GUARDS. Those from the hospital are being assisted. Even the stretcher cases are bundled into the vehicles, supervised by SUSAN and DR. VERSTAK. MRS. O'RIORDEN, on a stretcher, is loaded onto the truck.

SISTER WILHELMINA is fixing one of the truck engines, which the driver has not been able to start. As one of the GUARDS passes her a tool, she catches a glimpse of the INTERPRETER.

SISTER WILHELMINA

So. Vere do ve go now, Mr. Tomio?

He looks around, unwilling to answer; but then decides to risk it.

INTERPRETER

I don't know.

SISTER WILHELMINA

I think you do know.

INTERPRETER

Army man all crazy. I was schoolteacher in Osaka, then they tell me I am interpreter.

ADRIENNE

Tell us something, Mr. Tomio. Be a man.

The INTERPRETER looks around even more nervously. The trucks are being loaded and no one is paying any attention to him. He sweats with nerves.

INTERPRETER

General MacArthur back in Philippines. Chase Japanese soldier all over place.

He leaves quickly, afraid he has said too much. SISTER WILHELMINA signals to the DRIVER to start the engine. He presses the button and it roars into life. SISTER WILHELMINA turns to SUSAN, who is passing by with some people from the hospital.

SISTER WILHELMINA

My fader make me be a nun. Always want to be an engineer. Don't worry, I love God. Sometimes I just wonder what he's doing.

TOPSY is climbing into the truck. Her satin, and only, dress now a tattered remnant.

TOPSY

If my guys are coming, why don't Hirota and his gang just go and leave us here?

ROSEMARY

I don't know that they've ever done anything that made much sense.

THE NUNS, along with the younger and fitter members of the camp, are helping to load the sick from the hospital (DR. VERSTAK among them) into one of the trucks. A number of GUARDS stand by and watch as the WOMEN

89

struggle with the improvised stretchers up the backsteps of the vehicles. When one of the STRETCHER CARRIERS, carrying MRS. O'RIORDEN slips and falls, TWO of the GUARDS move forward to help, but a quick command from THE SNAKE makes them stop.

EXT. ROAD. EARLY MORNING.

The convoy of trucks moves quickly along the road.

EXT. TOWN. DAY.

The trucks move through the town of Palembang. They pass a large Colonial-style building with a Japanese flag flying. Some EUROPEAN WOMEN are on the verandah, but go back inside when they realize who is in the trucks.

INT. TRUCK. DAY.

SUSAN, ADRIENNE, MRS. O'RIORDEN, TOPSY, MISS DRUMMOND, and ROSEMARY look out through the damaged side wall of their truck. They see the WOMEN as they pass. BETT is among them.

                          SUSAN
    The satin sheet brigade.

                          TOPSY
    I knew I should have joined that bunch.

                    MRS. O'RIORDEN
    I think maybe we all should have.

MISS DRUMMOND smiles.

EXT. ROAD. DAY.

The trucks move along at high speed. There is forest on either side of the road. Occasional pedestrians leap out of the way.

INT. TRUCK. DAY.

The WOMEN are bounced around relentlessly. If not going from side to side they bounce up and down as large potholes are hit. MRS. ROBERTS groans in agony. Everyone is suffering, particularly all those moved from the hospital.

The GUARD indicates everyone is to push. The hill is steep, but bit by bit the truck gathers speed and then the engine kicks over. Everyone—WOMEN and GUARDS—clamber aboard.

The truck splutters its way over the crest of the hill and then picks up speed as it descends. The sun beats down fiercely and there is a rumble of distant thunder.

EXT. RAILWAY YARDS. DAY.

The trucks have stopped next to large tin buildings by a railway yard. The WOMEN climb out, exhausted, hungry, and thirsty, but are almost immediately pushed along by the side of the tracks toward a decrepit steam train. Most of the coaches are open goods trucks, though a couple of old passenger cars are at the end. It is a long walk. All of the sick have to be carried (which includes DR. VERSTAK, MRS. ROBERTS, and MISS DRUMMOND) and many (including MRS. O'RIORDEN) can only walk with support. A thunderstorm begins and lashes them with torrential rain.

HELEN and ROSEMARY sit against a pile of timber.

HELEN

Up dere (*she points to the distant mountains*) is de mountains at Loebok Lingau. My fader takes us dere in de summer. In de forest is many tigers. At night we close all der windows an' doors or dey come in der house. I lie in bed an' hear dem walk up and down the verandah. Pom . . . pom . . . So heavy dey are. I here dem breathe on de other side of der shutter. One morning I open de door and big tiger is asleep on der front step.

Thunder has been rumbling as HELEN spoke. Now a tropical downpour begins and soaks the two girls. Neither move.

ROSEMARY

I spent all my summers at my family's house in Dorset. No tigers, just rain—"soft days" we called them—and . . . that's where I met Dennis. We were 17 and he was my school friend's brother; I thought he was the best-looking boy I'd ever seen, but . . . it took so long for him to kiss me. I thought it was never going to happen. . . .

HELEN

And then it did?

ROSEMARY

Oh, yes, it did. We were in my father's study. I nearly fainted. We were so young—they didn't want us to see each other. So we pretended we weren't in love.

HELEN

So you keep seeing each other?

ROSEMARY

Yes. But we didn't fool anyone. I realized love is like a flame. It burns.
And it's visible to all.

The WOMEN climb up into the open rolling stock cars. The heavy rain makes
it all the more difficult.

Just as ROSEMARY and HELEN begin to climb up onto a rail car, ROSE-
MARY turns and sees a jeep driving along the roadway on the other side of
the tracks. It moves slowly because of the crowd. It contains FOUR JAPA-
NESE SOLDIERS. Between them, in the backseat, ROSEMARY sees her husband, DENNIS. He has been badly beaten and his head hangs forward.
ROSEMARY reacts with horror but is too astonished to be able to make any
noise at all. She watches the progress of the jeep as it continues on through
the crowd and out of sight.

EXT. COUNTRYSIDE. DAY.

Belching smoke, the train moves along through rice fields toward a distant
range of mountains.

EXT. TRAIN TRUCKS. DAY.

The WOMEN are jolted ceaselessly by the jerky motion of the train. It has
stopped raining but the trucks hold water to a depth of around six inches,
which sloshes around and over all the bodies trying to get some rest.

ADRIENNE nurses a sleeping MISS DRUMMOND. Nearby, SIOBHAN
and ARAN O'RIORDEN are comforted by SISTER WILHELMINA. HELEN
and ROSEMARY sit against the side of the truck, their arms around each
other. Both have been weeping.

MRS. O'RIORDEN quietly passes away.

EXT. TRAIN. DAY

The train travels slowly uphill along the lower slopes of the mountains. There
is dense forest on either side. It is now intensely hot.

EXT. TRAIN. NIGHT

With no lights showing, although the moon and stars are bright, the train
continues through the mountains of Sumatra.

EXT. COUNTRYSIDE. DAY.

The train continues through the densely forested landscape. The choir is singing "Londonderry Air."

EXT. FOREST STREAM. NEW CAMP. DAY.

Totally exhausted, the WOMEN wade through a shallow stream. Many of them are supporting one another; a couple of them are being carried on stretchers, including MRS. O'RIORDEN, whose face is now covered by a piece of cloth. HELEN is helping ROSEMARY, and ADRIENNE is supporting a weak MISS DRUMMOND, and CELIA and SUSAN are on either side of MRS. ROBERTS. SISTER WILHELMINA is holding the hands of SIOBHAN and ARAN.

Camera pans with them to reveal the new camp for the first time. It is a collection of decrepit buildings belonging to an old tin mine.

They enter the compound area. The Japanese have hastily erected a low-security barbed wire fence around the huts. On a rise beyond the huts is a large house, now also partially destroyed.

The WOMEN are too exhausted to take much notice of, or comment on, their surroundings. They enter the huts as quickly as possible to escape the heat and to seek rest.

INT. BUILDING. DAY.

The building is badly damaged with holes in the roof. There is no bedding, not even straw mats. Everyone is too exhausted to do anything else except find a spot to lie down for some rest. ROSEMARY and HELEN are in one another's arms. CELIA cradles her mother's head. TILLINGWORTH snuggles in beside them. ADRIENNE makes MISS DRUMMOND as comfortable as possible.

TOPSY
If I get out of this I'll never say another word against New Jersey.

ROSEMARY
(*softly*) But you'll never get out of this. None of us will ever leave Sumatra.

EXT. CAMP. NIGHT.

The camp is completely silent, except for the noises of the surrounding forest. No lights are visible.

EXT. COMPOUND. EARLY MORNING.

GUARDS are calling "Tenko." The WOMEN, dispirited, come out of the houses and line up. Even the CHILDREN have lost their sprightliness. AD-RIENNE assists the weak, failing MISS DRUMMOND.

INT. HOUSE. EARLY MORNING.

HELEN is trying to rouse ROSEMARY.

A number of women including MRS. ROBERTS, are too sick to be moved. CELIA is with her.

HELEN

Rosemary . . . don't give up now. Dennis vouldn't . . .

ROSEMARY

. . . wouldn't . . .

HELEN

. . . wouldn't want that . . . Rosemary . . . remember, vee are going to Lords to vatch the gentlemen's play cricket and den vee have tea . . . Rosemary . . .

ROSEMARY closes her eyes. HELEN watches her for a moment, then gets up when one of the GUARDS looks through the door.

EXT. COMPOUND. NIGHT.

The WOMEN are sitting around a small cooking fire, eating. The portions are tinier than ever before. SUSAN picks up a small fried blob. A grasshopper. She hesitates a moment, and then pops it into her mouth.

ADRIENNE

The snake isn't so bad.

SUSAN

The grasshoppers are delicious.

No one else is too enthusiastic about the snake. Everyone eats in silence. EDNA looks around rather wistfully.

EDNA

I wonder what Bing Crosby's up to now?

She addresses her remark to no one in particular.

ADRIENNE
Bing Crosby? Why?

EDNA
I miss him, that's all. Beaut, he is. Bing Crosby.

She begins to hum "Love Me Tonight."

MISS DRUMMOND
I must get the orchestra started again. Got to have a rehearsal.

ADRIENNE
Yes, of course, Margaret.

MISS DRUMMOND
Show the Japanese we're still alive. Got some spirit left.

MRS. PIKE
That bloody choir. You wouldn't be able to find enough people for a barbershop quartet.

MRS. DICKSON
Oh shut up, Harriet.

MRS. PIKE
Oh, shut up. You were bullied into joining by Adrienne.

MRS. DICKSON
That's true. Best thing that ever happened to me.

Once more silence falls. Each of them thinks longingly of the world outside the camp.

EXT. CAMP. DAY.

A high angle from one of the surrounding hills. The camp nestles at the foot of the valley.
 In a closer shot, WOMEN are up on the roofs, trying to repair the holes.

INT. HOSPITAL. DAY.

The atmosphere is somber. Among those seriously ill or dying are MRS. CRONJE and TWO of the NUNS.
 CELIA ROBERTS is trying to get her mother to eat something. She lifts her head and forces in a little food, but then MRS. ROBERTS' head falls back.

CELIA
Mummy, you have to eat something.

MRS. ROBERTS

You know . . . dear . . . I don't really mind dying. I've learned a great deal in the camps. I've . . . I did nothing, you know, in Singapore.

CELIA

Mummy, you're not going to die.

MRS. ROBERTS

Yes . . . I am . . . I'm only sorry I won't see your dear father . . . I would . . . have so much to tell him. So much to tell him.

Her voice trails away to a mumble. CELIA wipes her forehead, which is covered in sweat.

HELEN walks through the crowded hospital to the place where ROSEMARY is lying, sandwiched in between two other patients. She looks at ROSEMARY for a few moments. ROSEMARY'S face is covered in sweat and she is in a deep sleep.

HELEN looks around, then walks quickly up to DR. VERSTAK, who is standing with SUSAN at the other end of the room. DR. VERSTAK is malarial—she is wearing her overcoat and is leaning on a stick.

HELEN

Rosemary?

DR. VERSTAK looks around.

DR. VERSTAK

The beautiful English girl? Paradise Road.

She looks toward SUSAN.

SUSAN

Tomorrow, perhaps tonight.

DR. VERSTAK

Sometimes God reaches down and pulls der vings off his butterflies.

HELEN looks from DR. VERSTAK to SUSAN.

HELEN

What is it?

DR. VERSTAK

She doesn't want to live anymore. Perhaps now she realizes ze vorld is not a place vere lovers are reunited and good alvays vins.

DR. VERSTAK'S comments are not spoken unkindly but with an under-standably world-weary air.

HELEN

Her husband . . .

DR. VERSTAK

Ahhh, the great love affair . . . I can't say I'd pine away over any of my husbands.

HELEN

If I fall in love . . . (*she looks back toward Rosemary*) . . . then I hope it's like that.

DR. VERSTAK

Good luck, my dear.

EXT. JUNGLE CLEARING. MORNING.

MISS DRUMMOND with women.

MISS DRUMMOND

Father, in captivity we would lift our prayer to Thee.
Keep us ever in Thy love . . . Grant that daily we may prove those who
place their trust in Thee.
More than conquerors may be.
Give us patience to endure. Keep our hearts serene and pure.
Grant us courage, charity, greater faith, humility. . . .

The women around the graves throw flowers down.

MISS DRUMMOND

. . . readiness to own Thy will, be we free or captive still.
Amen.

WOMEN (*low chorus*)

Amen.

Rain falls on cross bearing name "R. Leighton-Jones."
Rain falls on cross bearing name "E. A. Roberts."
Graves with hill and huts behind.

EXT. BUILDING. DAY.

Rain falls from roof.
Guard stands under eaves.

EXT. COMPOUND. DAY.

Snails on grass. Hand picks them up.
   MRS. TIPPLER by fence collecting snails.
   SISTER WILHELMINA looks around.
   Hands pull snails from shells.
   SISTER WILHELMINA walks over.

SISTER WILHELMINA
What are you doing?

MRS. TIPPLER looks up.

MRS. TIPPLER
The French eat snails, don't they?

SISTER WILHELMINA
Yes, but I think those ones will make you sick.

MRS. TIPPLER eats a snail.
   SISTER WILHELMINA turns away.

INT. HOSPITAL. DAY.

ADRIENNE and OGGI enter the hospital hut. A large number of women are lying around, severely ill. SUSAN gestures to her. She goes to a section of the floor where MISS DRUMMOND is lying. She kneels beside her.

ADRIENNE
I'm here, Margaret. You can't die now. . . . Not now.

MISS DRUMMOND, emaciated, her face deathly pale and covered in sweat, mumbles incoherently. SUSAN mops her brow with a damp cloth. AD-RIENNE leans closer to try and catch what MISS DRUMMOND is saying.

SUSAN
Did you catch it? . . . She's asking for something. . . .

ADRIENNE nods.

ADRIENNE
I think so.

ADRIENNE takes MISS DRUMMOND'S hand in hers.

ADRIENNE

The Lord is my shepherd, I shall not want.
He maketh me to lie down in green pastures.
He leadeth me beside the still waters.
He restoreth my soul.
He leadeth me in the paths of righteousness
for His name's sake.
Yea, though I walk through the valley of the shadow of death
I will fear no evil: for Thou art with me.
Thy rod and thy staff, they comfort me.
Thou preparest a table before me,
in the presence of mine enemies,

ADRIENNE leans close to MISS DRUMMOND.

ADRIENNE

Thou anointest my head with oil;
My cup runneth over.
Surely goodness and mercy will follow me all the days of my life,
And I will dwell in the house of the Lord forever.

MISS DRUMMOND opens her eyes.

MISS DRUMMOND

That's what I wanted.

SUSAN

Amen.

MISS DRUMMOND closes her eyes.
ADRIENNE cries.

EXT. COMPOUND. NIGHT.

ADRIENNE is sitting by a small cooking fire. She has made a cross and is burning in the words "MARGARET DRUMMOND" with a screwdriver.

EXT. COMPOUND. EARLY MORNING.

THE SNAKE and other GUARDS are calling everyone out.

INT. HUTS. EARLY MORNING.

WOMEN drag themselves up once more.

As the WOMEN form the usual lines they begin to look around. SUSAN looks across the compound to see CAPTAIN TANAKA getting into a large and battered Japanese staff car. He looks back toward her, pauses, then gets in. The car drives off.

THE SNAKE and the other GUARDS are standing to one side. COLONEL HIROTA, followed by THE INTERPRETER, is walking toward a table and chair set up in the middle of the compound. ADRIENNE and SUSAN exchange a quizzical look. COLONEL HIROTA steps up onto the table. THE INTERPRETER moves forward to speak, but COLONEL HIROTA puts his hand up, indicating it is not necessary. He then speaks, in clear but halting English.

COLONEL HIROTA
The war . . . is over.

There is shocked silence. No one can cope with such a startling piece of news after so many years cut off from the outside world.

OGGI
(calling) Who won?

COLONEL HIROTA
Once more we can be . . . friend. I have done my best for you . . . I know it not enough . . . but I . . . do no more.

He gets down from his table and walks away, back toward his quarters. The other GUARDS hesitate for a moment, then follow him. The WOMEN stand silently a few seconds longer, then someone laughs. Another cheers. They begin embracing one another: SUSAN, ADRIENNE, HELEN, TOPSY, ANTOINETTE, SIOBHAN and ARAN O'RIORDEN, CELIA, MILLIE, DR. VERSTAK, MRS. DICKSON, SISTER WILHELMINA, etc. No one embraces MRS. TIPPLER.

TOPSY
Does this mean it's back to picking up the laundry and the groceries and all that? Oh, my God . . .

DR. VERSTAK
For you, darling. For me it vill be luxury hotels and limousine cars. Yes.

SUSAN catches her eye. They smile at one another. Around them the SURVIVORS are talking excitedly.

100

SUSAN

Are you really a doctor, Dr. Verstak?

DR. VERSTAK stands close to SUSAN.

DR. VERSTAK

Yes . . . and no . . . I know some medicine. My husband is a medical doctor. I am a doctor of philosophy. I hurt nobody. Maybe I help. Is wanting to survive so bad?

SUSAN turns and finds herself face to face with ADRIENNE.

ADRIENNE

Susan . . . dear Susan . . .

SUSAN

Adrienne . . .

They hug one another.

SUSAN

Well . . . we made it. . . .

ADRIENNE

Yes . . . we did . . . some of us . . .

Her eyes fill with tears.

As the WOMEN talk excitedly, the JAPANESE OFFICERS and GUARDS leave the compound. The gate is left open.

A title is superimposed, "24th August, 1945."

BRUCE BERESFORD was born in Australia and graduated from Sydney University in 1962. He served as Film Officer for the British Film Institute Production Board from 1966 through 1971, as well as acting as Film Advisor to the Arts Council of Great Britain. His 1975 film, *Dan's Party*, won Beresford the Best Director Award from the Australian Film Institute. His next film, *The Getting of Wisdom*, was selected for Director's Fortnight at the 1977 Cannes Film Festival. In 1982, Beresford received his second Academy Award nomination in the Best Director category for the film *Tender Mercies*, starring Robert Duvall. In 1987, Beresford's *Crimes of the Heart* was nominated for three Academy Awards. This film starred Diane Keaton, Jessica Lange, Sissy Spacek, and Sam Shepard. In 1990 *Driving Miss Daisy*, directed by Beresford, won four Academy Awards, including Best Picture and Best Actress for Jessica Tandy. The film was also selected as Best Film of the Year by the National Board of Review. Other film credits include: *Money Movers, The Club, Puberty Blues, Rich in Love, Silent Fall, Mister Johnson* (the first feature film to be shot entirely in Nigeria), and *Black Robe*. Beresford's *Last Dance*, starring Sharon Stone and Rob Morrow, will be released worldwide in late 1997.